TI
CTO | (
3X

Expanded And Updated

Building, Running and Changing
Tech Platforms, Teams and Careers

Rorie Devine

Copyright

The CTO ¦ CIO Bible 3X Revised, Expanded And Updated

First published 2023

Copyright © 2023 Rorie Devine

Version 1.0.

ASIN: B0CNPLT9DM

Contents

Key

👉 ❗ Key Points

🆔 Insight directly from my network

📖 Books definitely worth reading

🎢 Stories from the ups and downs of my career

💼 Case studies

🚩 Red Flags

Foreword

Selected by CIO.com as one of the "Best books for CIOs on Business Innovation and Leadership," *The CTO | CIO Bible* is for you if you're ambitious, in a hurry, and want to see the essence of being a successful CTO | CIO organised as super-concise, digital-friendly, bite-sized, chunks of actionable insight.

For people who appreciate deeper context, narrative, and real-world examples, *The CTO | CIO Bible* has been completely revised, updated, and expanded to create *The CTO | CIO Bible 3X*.

The CTO | CIO Bible 3X focuses on how to build, run, and change tech platforms, teams, and careers without, I hope, losing The CTO | CIO Bible's actionable insight density or diluting the much-liked approach of augmenting the narrative flow with top-tips, checklists, anecdotes, jokes, red flags, book recommendations, case studies and quotes from a number of successful leaders.

Hopefully, at least one "aha" moment is on each page of *The CTO | CIO Bible 3X*. Whether you are hoping to get promoted to CTO CIO one day, are a CTO CIO looking for a quick self or project health check, or are just a curious non-technical leader wanting to improve their understanding of the CTO CIO challenges and opportunities, *The CTO | CIO Bible 3X* is here to help you achieve your goals.

Introduction

In this CTO CIO Bible 3X, we'll look at "Doing The Right Thing" and then look at "Doing Things Right."

We'll start with how to build a tech platform and team, move on to how to run a tech platform and team, and then look at how to change a tech platform and team. We'll finish by taking an in-depth look at how to build a CTO CIO Career and personal brand before looking at how to run and change a CTO CIO Career and Personal Brand.

To me, leadership is about one thing: change. So, we will describe in detail what I call the Mission Objectives Strategies and Tactics (MOST) framework to help you create, structure, communicate, and execute your change initiatives and agendas.

In addition to exploring the processes of building, running, and changing tech platforms, teams, and careers, I will also discuss potential 'game changers' for your consideration. I'll delve into strategies for turning around under-performing teams, share insights on getting promoted to CTO or CIO, candidly revisit some of the biggest mistakes in my career, examine growth hacking, reflect on the characteristics of successful leadership, and provide links to an online hub containing templates, presentations, examples, and plans that you can utilise and adapt.

Many of the concepts discussed in this book apply equally to any leadership role in terms of the need to deliver business impact via your team and the tools available to you. However, leading a technology team also presents some specific challenges and opportunities that will be discussed.

In this book, we'll look at how to build, run, and change tech platforms, teams, and careers. But I won't be attempting to describe in depth *everything* possible to know about all of those subjects.

Not only would a book attempting to do that need to be unfeasibly large, but it would almost certainly be out-of-date by the time it was written.

Instead of describing common practice and standard approaches, I will focus on "gotchas," traps for the unwary, hacks, and interesting/unusual tools, techniques, and approaches that current and future tech leaders might want to consider.

French philosopher and mathematician Blaise Pascal "I would have written a shorter letter, but I did not have the time."

Also new for *The CTO / CIO Bible 3X* is creating an online knowledge hub containing links to templates, presentations, blog posts, etc., on the subjects being discussed.

Anyway, without further ado, let's get cracking.

Section 1: Building a Tech Platform And Team

Building A Tech Platform

We normally inherit rather than build tech platforms and teams, but what makes a tech platform good or bad? How should we evaluate it?

Which high-level principles should we apply if we are lucky enough to be building or unlucky enough to be re-platforming a tech platform?

Fundamentally, a tech platform or architecture should

- Facilitate the delivery of the company's business plan
- At the lowest possible cost
- Whilst introducing the minimum number of constraints

What Makes A Good Tech Platform?

After a recent one-hour outage, Elon Musk took to Twitter to complain about how "brittle" the Twitter platform was.

So, how should we architect a tech platform to maximise effectiveness and introduce the minimum number of constraints?

A good, effective, flexible tech architecture should be:

- As simple as possible, non-brittle, and easy to change
- Horizontally and vertically scalable
- Resilient with no single points of failure

- Tiered with good separation of responsibilities and concerns
- Secure by design

In general, horizontal scalability means adding additional servers/compute power to a layer whilst vertical scalability increases the computing power of individual servers/modules.

Ensure that every action within your architecture is authenticated and logged. Encrypt all data in transit and at rest, establish a robust perimeter, and make it impossible to navigate freely within different areas.

It's very beneficial to create asynchronous rather than synchronous functionality and architectures.

An asynchronous operation is a type of operation where the task being performed runs separately from the main thread of execution. This means that the operation does not block or wait for the operation to complete before moving on to other tasks.

This approach avoids blocking/locking the user/requestor and the resource being used. If a synchronous approach is taken, your capacity is fixed at the number of resources you can make available in parallel and is easily overwhelmed in surge situations like DDoS attacks.

Asynchronous operations can be implemented in various ways, including using threads, callbacks, promises, and coroutines.

☞ An architecture is considerably more resilient and flexible if it is impotent. An idempotent architecture, on the other hand, is one that doesn't maintain state. In other words, an operation doesn't need to know what happened before it was applied and can safely be applied multiple times without unintended side effects.

Separation of concerns

Separation of concerns is a design principle in software engineering that suggests that a software system should be divided into distinct modules or components, each responsible for a separate and distinct aspect of the system's functionality. In other words, each module should be concerned with only one specific task or responsibility and not be concerned with any other aspect of the system.

❗ A good example of separation of concerns is having *different* permanent data stores for data read and write operations. They are very different use cases and can be implemented and optimised differently and effectively.

There are different ways to achieve separation of concerns, depending on the nature of the system and the programming language or technology being used.

Some common techniques include using design patterns, such as the Model-View-Controller (MVC) pattern, or using interfaces and abstractions to decouple different parts of the system.

From top to bottom, a simplified platform architecture might look something like this;

- User interfaces
- API
- Services layer
- Storage

Let's look at each of these in more detail.

User interfaces

Apps, websites, speech interfaces, and more—ideally, user interfaces should contain zero business logic. Their primary focus should be on delivering effective, rich, and engaging user experiences.

As CTO CIO, you should have zero tolerance for implementing business logic anywhere outside the core services created to implement your business logic. If the business logic is hardcoded in apps or wherever, it will mean that any changes to the business logic will need to be implemented more than once, and inconsistent business logic and customer experiences are inevitable.

Put your business logic in microservices behind an API. You will live to regret any other approach one day.

API: Build all of the user interfaces on a public API from the get-go. A public API is a huge asset and strategic capability for any company, allowing it to offer its products and services both B2B and B2C much more easily.

When I look at the companies I've worked for that have been very successful, one common denominator is that they have all utilised public APIs to enable both B2C and B2B revenue streams and business models.

Version your API so that you can simultaneously use different versions of your API with different partners. This will help avoid functionality conflict between different partners and enable easy upgrade paths.

Microservices layer

All of your business logic should be on your servers, broken down into microservices.

A microservices architecture is an approach to building software applications as a collection of small, independent services that communicate with each other through well-defined APIs.

Overall, microservices architecture can provide a number of benefits for software development, including scalability, flexibility, resilience, faster development, easier maintenance, improved collaboration, and better fault isolation.

For Matt and Boyan's great presentations on microservices, see The Hub gro.team/cto-cio-bible-3X/hub/

Don't overdo a microservices decomposition and break functionality into too many services. There is a definite overhead in creating and managing a set of services, which grows more than linearly as the number of services grows.

The Goldilocks zone for microservices (not too many, not too few, just right) might be breaking down your platform into services that are:

- Independent (i.e., ideally not dependent on other services)

- Responsible for fulfilling a single specific business need (e.g., registration)

- Optimised for their individual use case (using the best technology for that job, e.g., Node.js v golang)

! Having a set of 100% orthogonal services probably won't be possible in the real world. You'll need to apply a bit of pragmatism. Create your services into blocks of functionality that just seem to make sense and feel right. If functionality is duplicated more than 3-5 times in the services, then maybe it would be better to break it out into its own service.

! At Hailo, we initially made the mistake of over-decomposing our functionality down into 230 'ish very "micro" microservices. The friction of managing and debugging so many small services proved significant, so we composed some of the services back up again to some degree. Creating the services as singular logical business operations such as registration seemed to be the sweet spot for us.

Storage

Underneath (when viewed on a typical IT architecture diagram anyway) the microservices are usually the permanent data storage layers. These are typically SQL databases, no SQL databases, block storage, etc.

! There really is no excuse or need for an IT architecture to be dependent on a single SQL database these days. Due to their shared memory architecture, SQL data-bases are comparatively slow, relatively difficult/expensive to scale/replicate, and often single points of failure. Much better approaches are discussed later.

As Sanjay Jadhav (a CTO/CSO/CPO) says, "The most important thing about being a Tech Leader is that he/she should be well aware of their domain landscape and where the industry & technology needs to be steered towards. The leader should have good business acumen, be data & security oriented, be a people person, and be a thought leader in his/her domain."

Server-side languages

You want to be on the leading edge, not the bleeding edge, of the technology adoption curve. If you adopt the first versions of things, you will probably end up in a world of pain. It's a balance, though. You will be left behind if you adopt emerging technologies too slowly. Evaluate every opportunity on a case-by-case basis and learn as much as possible from other people's real-world experiences.

The direction of travel seems to be to move everything back to the server side these days. Of course, we began on the client side with HTML/JavaScript and then transitioned everything to the server side with ASP/JSP. Subsequently, we reverted to the client side. Now, leveraging Next.js and server actions for performance, security, and SEO reasons, we find ourselves moving back to the server side. Oh well, everything changes, yet everything stays the same.

At the time of writing, I think the best back-end language comes down to a choice of one or both Node.js and/or golang.

☞ Node.js is great for most early-stage company/team use cases, with golang coming into its own when the number of customers, transactions, or developers starts scaling up.

☞ It'd be nice if all of the services were written in the same language. But there is nothing wrong with using Scala, Node, and so on as the primary language, with something like golang being used for the super-intensive tasks, in my opinion.

JavaScript

JavaScript truly is 'eating the world.' After managing to avoid writing it for all these years, I recently 'bit the bullet' and learned to write it. I must admit I'm very impressed with its power and flexibility, but I still dislike its 'hacky' syntax. Getting all the packages to play nicely together requires a lot of Stack Overflow usage.

Node.js

The server-side version of JavaScript is a flexible and accessible server-side language. Being single-threaded and interpreted isn't as fast or scalable as languages like golang. However, sharing a syntax with the most popular front-end language makes it a good choice for many use cases.

Google Go golang

Even if you're not particularly interested in server-side computer languages, the following more detailed section is a good example of the sort of technology features and attributes you might want to consider when evaluating new technologies.

Why could Go, a.k .a. golang, be your weapon of choice as a server-side language?

Go, also known as Golang, is an open-source programming language that originated at Google in 2007. It was developed by Robert Griesemer, Rob Pike, and Ken Thompson. In the realm of programming languages, it's relatively new (especially compared to Java, which has been around since 1995, and PHP since 1994). Nevertheless, Robert, Rob, and Ken have successfully integrated the best ideas from various existing languages. As an open-source project, it is essentially free to use, and Google reports that more than half of the check-ins on the project now come from contributors outside of Google.

I didn't have any golang developers at Hailo when I decided to migrate to it, so our existing PHP and Java developers had to learn it "on the job." With a few exceptions, they took to it like "a duck to water" and usually did their first check-in by the end of their first two-week sprint.

Golang is easier to write and manage than Java. It runs faster than almost everything except C or C++. Because it scales across multiple cores or CPUs in a server "out of the box," you can save money using fewer servers.

Faster

Go is a compiled language that compiles the source code programmers write down to the binary language servers can execute without further translation.

This differs from the interpreted languages like PHP, Python, or Ruby, which need to run on top of software interpreters. This makes Go significantly quicker in a straight line than scripting languages. (It's not even that much of a problem that you must compile your code before running it. The run command compiles and runs your go code so quickly that it's like working with a scripting language).

Go is so blisteringly fast that it is now being used to write many of the components underpinning the leading-edge digital architectures. Docker (the market-leading virtualisation technology) is written in Go, as is NSQ (the rock-solid messaging platform), Bitly, and so on...

Easier

Go is object-based (rather than object-orientated like Java) and has none of the fiddly memory management and pointer things you need to keep on top of in C++.

Because it compiles down to a binary, executing Go code is as simple as deploying a file to a server and running it. There are no libraries, frameworks, or interpreters to worry about.

Some people think the Go compiler is a little too fussy (it will complain if you include a library and don't use it, for instance). But in combination with Go being a strongly typed language

(I won't open that can of worms here), the upshot is that more errors are usually found at compile time rather than at run time – and we'd much rather see any errors than our customers did.

Cheaper

Go's killer feature is its concurrency model. Out of the box, it will automatically create code that utilises multiple cores or CPUs by creating parallel executing threads. This is how companies like Hailo and Dropbox have achieved dramatic scalability improvements by moving to Go.

With interpreted languages like Python, JavaScript, Ruby, PHP, etc., even if they are technically multi-threaded, only one thread can ever execute at one time (because of the Global Interpreter Lock).

Hailo accidentally found themselves as AWS's biggest customer in Europe by launching in more than 20 new cities by duplicating the London system and changing the city name to New York. We reduced the AWS bill by more than 50% by re-platforming to Hailo 2.0 (or H2O), a global Go-based microservices platform. For more on Hailo, see Matt and Boyan's decks in The Hub gro.team/cto-cio-bible-3X/hub/

The ease with which your team can spin up environments in the cloud is both a strength and a weakness. You can find that cloud hosting bills are much higher than you expect due to zombie instances and instance bloat. Encourage your team to develop skills in tools like AWS Terraform to script environment creation and destruction and stand down environments when they are not utilised.

Does golang have any downsides?

There is no such thing as a "good" or "bad" computer language; they all have strengths and weaknesses, and you need to work back from the problem you're trying to solve before deciding which language is optimum for your particular circumstances.

Golang is state of the art for use cases like back-end API and micro services frameworks where you want low response times and hosting bills. But it isn't designed for the user interface layer: JavaScript is eating that particular world.

Golang's relative newness also means there aren't as many libraries (chunks of code you can include and use) as existing for other languages. Good open-source citizens like Dropbox are writing and open-sourcing any missing ones as we speak.

While there aren't as many Golang programmers in the market compared to other languages, at Hailo, we discovered that the opportunity to use Golang attracted a sufficient number of talented programmers. Almost all of our PHP and Java developers found it easy to learn and become productive in Golang. The dual naming (Go and Golang) might be a bit confusing, and the Gopher logo is a little odd, but I'm nit-picking now.

In my experience, a back-end platform written in Go will probably be quicker, easier, and cheaper than all the current alternatives. But a lot really will depend on your business needs.

Not every business wants or needs minimised response times and maximised scalability. The cost of migrating an existing API or Platform is far from free, of course.

📖 *Elon Musk: Tesla, SpaceX, and the Quest for a Fantastic Future* by Ashlee Vance as an honest view of one of the most significant entrepreneurs of our time. Apparently, Elon had agreed to sell Tesla to Google before the employees came through on his request to sell three Tesla cars each. Did you know that Elon founded OpenAI of ChatGPT fame as well? He may issue a lawsuit after his $1 Billion investment into a "non-profit" company was used to create the very "for-profit" Microsoft-backed OpenAI we had/have today.

Serverless Architectures

Serverless architecture is a type of computing architecture in which a cloud provider manages the infrastructure and automatically allocates computing resources as needed to execute small, self-contained functions in response to specific events or triggers.

In a serverless architecture, developers write and deploy code in the form of functions, which are typically small pieces of code that perform a specific task. When a function is triggered, the cloud provider automatically provisions the necessary resources to run it, executes it, and then releases the resources when it is complete.

This approach eliminates the need for developers to manage the underlying infrastructure, such as servers or virtual machines. It allows them to focus on writing code.

The ease at which developers can create serverless architectures is a strength and weakness. They are quick and easy to spin up, which means they are generally used for use cases when traditional servers would be significantly cheaper and more appropriate.

Examples of serverless computing services include AWS Lambda, Azure Functions, and Google Cloud Functions.

While serverless architectures have some advantages, there are also major downsides to consider:

Cold start issues: Serverless functions may have a "cold start" delay when invoked, resulting in slow response times. This is because the cloud provider needs to spin up a new instance of the function to handle the request.

I was once involved in a project that had to replace a serverless architecture because the serverless cold start delays (which can be up to one second) were causing data inconsistency and data loss problems. In computing terms, one second is an age (see The Biggest Mistakes Of My Career)

Limited control: With serverless architectures, the cloud provider manages the underlying infrastructure, and you have limited control over it. This can make it difficult to debug issues or optimise performance.

Increased complexity: Serverless architectures can be more complex to set up and manage than traditional server-based architectures. They often involve multiple services and APIs that need to be integrated and managed.

Vendor lock-in: Serverless implementations are platform-specific. Once you start using a specific cloud provider's serverless platform, switching to a different provider can be difficult without significant rework.

Higher cost: While serverless architectures can be cost-effective for certain workloads, they can also be far more expensive than traditional server-based architectures for certain types of workloads.

Serverless approaches can cost ten times more than other approaches.

Overall, serverless architectures can be a powerful tool for prototypes, POCs, or spiky and infrequent workloads. However, they may not be the best fit for all production use cases. It's important to carefully consider the trade-offs and potential downsides before creating a serverless architecture.

Event-Driven Architectures

An event-driven architecture (EDA) is a type of computing architecture in which software components communicate with each other by triggering events rather than invoking methods or functions. In this architecture, events are generated by various components or services. They are processed asynchronously by other components or services that have subscribed to those events.

In an event-driven architecture, events are published to a central event bus or message broker, which acts as a hub for routing events to the appropriate subscribers. Subscribers can then process the events and take appropriate actions, such as sending notifications, updating databases, or triggering other events.

Apache Kafka is a mature and reliable event streaming platform. Events are published as topics, and systems connect asynchronously to subscribe to the topics they are interested in.

One of the main benefits of an event-driven architecture is its ability to enable loosely coupled, scalable systems. Services can be added or removed without disrupting the overall system, and the architecture can handle large volumes of events without the need for complex synchronisation or locking mechanisms.

Building A Tech Platform Recap

A good tech platform should enable efficient delivery of a company's business plan with minimal cost and constraints.

It should be simple, non-brittle, scalable horizontally and vertically, resilient, well-tiered for separation of responsibilities, and secure by design, including authentication and encryption.

Asynchronous operations are beneficial over synchronous ones for avoiding bottlenecks, especially in high-traffic situations.

Separation of concerns is crucial, with distinct layers for user interfaces, APIs, services, and storage; business logic should reside in microservices behind APIs.

The right server-side technologies, like Node.js or Go, should be chosen based on the balance between innovation and performance, and architectures like serverless and event-driven should be considered based on specific needs and trade-offs.

Building a Tech Team

The single biggest factor affecting your likelihood of success as a CTO CIO is the amount and quality of talent you have at your disposal.

Do you have the people with the domain knowledge you need?

Do you have people with the right attitude?

Do you have people and teams that can deliver at the cadence you need to deliver your objectives?

Hiring Tech People

If you need to hire, you should hire across what I call the three axes of hiring:

- Domain expertise
- Impact focus
- Being a team player

Many hiring mistakes have been made when hiring engineers by solely looking at domain expertise...

Don't make the mistake of setting the hiring bar so high that very few people get hired. I have seen many teams struggle because nobody could ever match their unrealistically high hiring standards...

We want the best talent possible, so we need to take an optimistic approach. If you're 50:50 on someone, give them a chance. Probation periods exist to facilitate paperwork-light exits if a hire doesn't ultimately work out.

While working at a business undergoing layoffs after a financial crash, I noticed that one role seemed to have less impact compared to others. However, whenever I proposed making this role redundant, the CEO pushed back, stating that the person in that role was always the last one left in the office in the evening. It later turned out that the individual was running his Indian offshoring company from our office overnight!

It's sometimes hard as a human being, but try to make sure that you objectively evaluate people and teams in terms of their business impact, and not less rational and relevant considerations such as tenure, sociability, relationships, etc.

Given a choice, I'd rather run a smaller team of more talented people than a larger team of less talented people. The costs may be the same, but in my experience, the smaller team will deliver more.

Modern HR frameworks like Workleap Officevibe can help measure and manage your team's engagement and morale. By polling the team every week, they can create a dashboard showing you metrics and trends in things like "engagement," "alignment," and so on. The anonymous feedback aspects of systems like this can create Twitter-like trolling. Sometimes, it's hard not to try to work out who is saying what.

Being creative on office hours, working from home arrangements, office/remote locations, and embracing interim vs. permanent arrangements may unlock the door to getting the talent you need to be successful.

There are no 'perfect' ways to manage performance and compensation; all approaches are imperfect and flawed in their own way. Ultimately, if the team feels that the approach is fair and as objective as possible, they will choose to over-look the real-world imperfections and inconsistencies inherent in whatever approach is being taken.

A person's compensation needs to reflect their contri-bution to the team and company. You may get away with paying someone under the market rate for their abilities and value for a while. But you will eventually get found out, and you will lose them.

OKRs And Performance Management Frameworks

There are no perfect performance management frameworks. They are all flawed to some extent, pri-marily because it's challenging for one human being to encapsulate the objective value and contribution of another human being as a set of numbers, especially in creative roles like software development.

Frameworks like OKRs are inconsistent with the principles of Agile development. Specifying what you want a team to deliver for the next 3-6 months is more aligned with Water-fall methodologies and not Agile at all.

Popularised by Google, quarterly OKRs (Objectives and Key Results) are probably the most commonly used performance management framework.

If you're running a high number of independent self-organising teams (say more than 10), then you'll need some sort of framework to "herd the cats," so if you are going to use OKRs.

- 3-5 OKRs per quarter seems about right in practice; too many or too few leads to sub-optimal outcomes.
- Make sure the key results are SMART (Specific, Measurable, Achievable, Relevant, and Time-bound), ideally binary success/failure measures. Having to argue with team members whether a KR has been achieved is a massive lose-lose.
- Use a mix of individual, team, and company OKRs. Indeed, some (particularly more junior) individuals won't be able to directly impact company performance so much, but business is a team game.
- Use company OKRs to "walk the walk" by focusing on independent measures of performance and clearly making the link between individual compensation and company performance. Individual comp can't be inconsistent with overall company performance.

If plans change (and they always do), the OKRs should also be updated. Few companies bother to do this, which turns the whole OKR process into a "box ticking" exercise.

Incentive And Compensation Frameworks

Given the imperfections of performance management frameworks like OKRs, I can understand why HR people are reluctant to tie comp directly to them. However, separating compensation from goal-setting frameworks can create as many problems as it solves.

Suppose compensation isn't tied directly to a performance management framework. In that case, you will have to create and run a separate, parallel compensation and reward process.

This creates a whole new set of problems, of course. If there is a separate compensation framework, the team will care much more about the outcome of the compensation process than the OKRs. How do you make sure the separate frameworks are consistent?

If I had a blank sheet of paper, my compensation framework would look something like this.

- There would be no fixed date team/company cycle. Comp and performance would be reviewed for each person on the first anniversary of their joining date and reviewed annually after that
- If I was running more than 10 independent self-organising product development teams, I would use a goal-setting framework like OKRs; otherwise, I wouldn't waste everyone's time
- I would be able to manage individual compensation proactively by increasing people's comp if/when their contribution

increases, without waiting for an annual performance review cycle or a perception that they have become a flight risk.

- Every year, each member of the team would be invited to self-assess their performance over the previous year, and their line manager would do the same
- The line manager would recommend a compensation increase for the person based on the average increase agreed for the team linked to current company performance. The recommended increase would be independently reviewed
- If the median increase for the team is X%, high per-formers should be awarded X+10%, median performers X% and under-performers 0%.

Getting rid of a calendar-fixed annual performance review process would also help smooth out churn, of course. Churn is always highest in the quarter following the performance review process.

One way to get a good view of your talent map is to ask your team what they think via 1 on 1 individual interview (which is covered later). In my experience, group sessions aren't very effective in this area as people are less willing to speak frankly in public forums.

You can't realistically shape your strategies and tac-tics until you have a feel for the talent you have at your disposal and what talent you may need to bring in.

I often find frustration working with "old school" colleagues in Security, Compliance, or Finance who default to saying "No!" When hiring for these roles, it's crucial to carefully assess the right attitude. Their response to a business initiative should not be "We can't do that for security/compliance/cost reasons," but rather, "Great... let's find a way to achieve that despite the security/compliance/financial challenges."

We had a company performance bonus scheme with success/failure at one company based on the company hitting 30% revenue growth. One year, we were only tracking 29% revenue growth. But after some soul searching, some revenue was found "down the back of the sofa" to hit 30% revenue growth and pay the bonus.

Everyone says hiring the best talent possible is the most important thing, and they're right. But you need a spectrum of talent in every team. Not all of a team's responsibilities are cool, interesting, or ground-breaking, so a team consisting solely of high performers would struggle to keep everyone equally challenged and motivated.

From day one, an important facet of the team culture you create should be that everyone feels safe speaking up, being involved, and contributing. Keep an eye on how and how often people in the team communicate (Slack analytics can help with this). You want to see frequent and cross "border" team communication. It's a red flag if individuals or teams aren't communicating with their colleagues as much as everyone else.

The Organisation And Structure Of An Engineering Team

I like to use a tried and tested core DR team structure when creating a tech team:

- CTO | CIO | VP Engineering
- Software Delivery Director/VP
- Service Delivery Director/VP
- Information Security Director/VP
- Head of Architecture

Fit the structure to the team, not the team to the structure. In other words, the structure is a "How," not a "What." The right people will do a good job, whatever the structure is. Getting the right people in the team and around the table is much more important than their job titles/roles.

At Yell, I used an "Office of the CTO" to help communicate and coordinate the "V3" change initiative. The people involved (Nicola and Julia) were very good, so I think it was part of why the team transformation was achieved so successfully.

The Head Of Architecture Role

Once the team's architecture and platform reach a certain size or complexity, such as having more than 30 people in the Tech Team or creating a public API, having someone focused inward, overseeing the overall consistency and coherence of the software and cloud/API architecture, can be very valuable.

As the software delivery teams become more independent and self-organising, having an architect to help them architect their software coherently can pay big dividends. (A Thin Client → API → Services architecture pattern also helps keep things simple and coherent, of course).

The Head of Architecture role is one of the most challenging roles in a tech team. A good head of architecture needs to be a deep technologist and a great collaborator. Good architects are like "gold dust" and don't tend to change jobs very often.

The Head Of Security Role

Once the company's financial or reputational "value at risk" is worth protecting, having a specialist Head Of Security is worthwhile. The security threat landscape is growing and changing very quickly, so having a full-time subject matter expert to mitigate the risks can help everyone sleep better at night.

Integrating Offshore, Remote, and In-House Teams

As a CTO CIO, you will need different types of software delivery capability.

- Core product/service delivery

- Additional product/service delivery

- Platform capability delivery

Your core product/service is how you deliver your value proposition to your customers. So you will want to collocate the product and tech teams working on this as closely to the company's "centre of gravity" as possible.

Additional product/service delivery is for things that aren't necessarily core to the business but round out and enhance the overall value proposition.

Platform capability comprises elements necessary for creating a holistic user experience, such as payment processing. These elements are common across businesses and may not necessarily provide a competitive advantage for the company.

At Betfair, we located the core product/service teams in the Hammersmith HQ. We worked with variable capacity project-based partners to create additional products/services and created an off shore team in Romania to create and manage the payment rails.

Setting up an offshore development team in Cluj, Romania, was hugely successful for Betfair. The team survived and thrived and has grown to be more than 1,000 people.

How To Explore And Choose New Technologies

As CTO CIO, you should always be looking for ways to create a competitive advantage for your company, so you must actively keep an eye on emerging technologies and track them as they ascend the maturity curve from bleeding edge to leading edge.

Maintain a dialogue with your team and peers about emerging tech on Slack or wherever. Twitter, blogs, podcasts, and so on are all great places to learn about emerging technologies. Keep up a watching brief for opportunities to make things quicker, better, and cheaper for your company.

When selecting technology for the new Hailo 2.0 platform, we adopted a unique approach: we chose a technology capability per two-week sprint (e.g., Sprint 1 = message queue technology, Sprint 2 = data store, Sprint 3 = server-side language, and so on). In each sprint, a volunteer selected a technology they found interesting and demonstrated how much working software they could create with it by the end of the sprint. It was a collaborative process, and in most cases, there was a clear winner, as some technologies didn't live up to their hype. (Spoiler alert: we chose Go/golang as the server-side language).

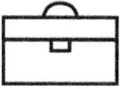

Case Study: Quicker, Better, Cheaper Product Development

Outcome:

A new website was launched for 50% of the cost and 33% of the time of previous approaches.

Context:

At GRO.TEAM, we haven't had entirely satisfactory experiences the last few times we have commissioned website/app builds through the traditional routes. Hence, we decided to "eat our own dog food" for our website relaunch and asked an Interim CPTO to set up a virtual project team to get our new website built and launched.

Approach:

The Interim CPTO assembled a hand-picked virtual project team comprising UX/UI (Cyprus), Front End (Pakistan), Back End (UK) and DevOps (India) in late May and off they went. The talent was sourced through Fiverr and existing relationships.

Results:

The costs were less than 50% of the previous website build, and it took 33% of the time. The organic SEO impressions also increased by 350%, and the organic clicks increased by 750%.

Key Lessons Learnt:

- Assembling a hand-picked team of "10X" engineers can result in quicker, better and cheaper delivery.

Make sure the project leader is trustworthy and of high calibre.

Building A Tech Team Recap

The success of a CTO/CIO heavily relies on the talent and quality of the team, considering their domain knowledge, attitude, and delivery pace.

Hiring should balance three axes: domain expertise, impact focus, and teamwork, and avoid setting unattainable hiring standards.

Compensation should align with individual contributions, and whilst performance management frameworks like OKRs are imperfect, for large teams, they help align individual, team, and company goals.

A tech team's organisation should be adaptable, with roles like Head of Information Security and Head of Architecture becoming crucial as complexity increases.

Integrating diverse delivery capabilities (collocated, variable, offshore) and maintaining awareness of emerging technologies is vital for a CTO/CIO to stay competitive.

Section 2: Running A Tech Platform And Team

Running a Tech Platform

As I say multiple times in this book, don't make the mistake of neglecting your day-to-day operational responsibilities, keeping the "lights on" and the money coming in when considering the future.

Delivering a great product or service today earns you a seat at the table to talk about the products or services you could/should deliver tomorrow.

No Staging Environment

I'm a firm supporter of the point that there are much better ways to de-risk software quality and live production availability risks these days than by using a Staging environment.

Theoretically, a replica production environment on which to perform final software/hardware testing and checks before upgrading the production environment sounds like a great idea. However, in reality, and unfortunately, the direct and indirect costs generally exceed the benefits.

The downsides of using a Staging environment

1. To fulfill its raison d'etre, Staging needs to consist of identical hardware and software to Production. Achieving this, especially in the cloud, is very difficult and often expensive wherever attempted.
2. For effective testing, the data in Staging must be identical to Production. Replicating data between systems is

always imperfect, difficult, and expensive, regardless of how frequently it is attempted.

3. Managing Staging requires as much time and effort as managing Production when done properly. In high-level terms, let's estimate that setting up a Staging environment decreases DevOps productivity by 30-50%.

As usual, there are no absolutely correct or incorrect approaches. It's a question of evaluating the trade-offs.

If I were running a nuclear power station with human lives at risk, I would probably use a Staging environment.

For other, less critical use cases, a better approach is available.

Testing In Production (TIP)

Testing in production is one of those practices that divides opinion, with people being both pro and anti.

The advances in traffic shaping and deployment/roll back automation software have made TIP viable and preferable in most use cases.

Given the complex dependencies in contemporary production systems (and numerous potential edge cases), production testing has become essential for DevOps and software development.

Leading software enterprises like Google, Netflix, and Amazon now regularly avoid a "big bang" by rolling out new features to a subset of their user traffic.

Hailo was a global "Uber using licensed taxis" app, so realistically, simulating production data and activity in a test system was impossible once we were live in 20 cities from Japan to the USA. A better approach was needed. Our test engineer, Jono, created a live Hailo city on the pacific island of Kerguelen, which is actually entirely populated by penguins. Jono created some robot taxis to drive around picking up the penguins, and voila, we had a live city on which we could perform continuous testing and monitoring. Using this approach, we could know immediately if a deployment has caused unintended issues, and it would be rolled back before it had affected real passengers.

(for more on Hailo, see Matt and Boyen's decks in The Hub gro.team/cto-cio-bible-3X/hub/)

Managing Technical Debt

One of the more challenging aspects of running a technology platform is managing technical debt.

We can define "Tech debt" as sub-optimal hardware or software that needs refactoring or replacing because it makes things slower, more difficult, or expensive.

It is usually either "legacy" code that is past its "sell by date" or newer code that was implemented in a "quick and dirty" way due to a deadline and time-to-market being prioritised over future maintainability/scalability.

In certain types of situations, "quick and dirty" is absolutely the right thing to do. As long as everyone is explicitly aware of the "costs" of going down this path and of remediating the situation in the future, then everything will work out fine.

👉 We normally don't have the luxury of telling our business that we need to rework/redo something, so they should leave us alone until we tell them that we've finished. However, LinkedIn did exactly that when it paused product development for two months in 2013 to implement Continuous Integration and Continuous Deployment (CI/CD).

The best way of managing tech debt is to make everything explicit.

Make any negative velocity or other impacts the tech debt is causing very explicit so a business knows the "tax" it is paying in terms it can understand. Increased business understanding and awareness can only help ensure that the right trade-off decisions are made when the tech debt needs to be addressed and so on.

Similarly, make any "quick and dirty" implementation trade-offs explicit. "We can do it this way in X days, but it will have a negative impact of A per B per sprint until changed, or we can do it in this other way in Z days with no ongoing overhead."

❗ The optimum way of dealing with tech debt is to address it when an area of the codebase is being changed to add new features or functionality. Make the costs and benefits of doing this explicit.

🎢 When I walked into Hailo, the tech team was about to quit "en masse" because they were fed up with launching Hailo cities by cloning a whole AWS stack and changing London to Dublin or whatever. (This is a good way to end up as AWS's biggest customer in Europe, of course). Needless to say, this approach was not sustainable and was one reason we had to re-platform to Hailo 2.0.

Managing A Technology Team Budget

These days, the biggest technology team expenses are normal people, followed by cloud provider costs, with everything else some way down the list.

In some ways, things are much simpler now, but there is also less flexibility.

It's hard to save money in the margins on people costs. Likewise, cloud providers don't really provide flexible pricing or discounts.

Using AWS reserved instances can save you around 5-10% on their bills, but you're effectively pre-paying for the privilege.

Watch out for significant price increases if your SaaS provider is acquired or receives significant venture capital investment. The real red flag is when the pricing on their website changes from $X per Y to "Call Sales." As soon as some SaaS providers get to a certain size, they think they're SAP/Oracle and start trying to use lock-in to price-gouge their customers.

Some SaaS providers deliberately leave it until 6-8 weeks before the expiry of your annual contract before popping up and asking for more money so that you won't realistically have time to migrate off their system before the expiry of the contract.

Once SaaS providers move away from publicly quoted role/usage-based prices, we know that Salespeople just make the prices up based on what they think they can get away with. We know that...and they know we know that.

Proactively manage your contracts and renewals and make sure that you flag any supplier risks to your stake-holders. Ensure you have a genuine contingency plan thought through and cost ready for if/when a supplier becomes a risk due to cost or some other reason. When negotiating with sup-pliers, they need to think that you could genuinely migrate off their services if they push you too far into win/lose territory.

Capex v Opex

CFOs generally hate fixed Capital Expenditure Capex costs and prefer variable Operating Expenses or Opex Costs. A CFO would really need to write this section. But it's not as simple as Opex = good, Capex = bad because Opex hits the P&L, certain Capex accounting treatments don't, and in some states/countries, certain types of Capex can be claimed against schemes like R&D tax credits.

Make a point of talking to your CFO to really under-stand what the optimum Opex/Capex mix is for your business/team over the next 12-24 months. In the UK, R&D tax credits, for instance, can be material.

Developing On Main/Trunk Based Development

"Developing on main," also known as "trunk-based development," is another approach attracting both very "pro" and "anti" schools of thought.

It refers to the practice in software development where developers directly make changes to the 'main' branch (also known as the 'master' branch in some version control systems) of a code repository.

This approach is contrasted with creating long-lived separate branches for new features or fixes, which is considered a best practice in most modern development workflows.

For teams at the right stage of maturity and capability, I have found that developing on main is a net positive, increasing velocity and helping prevent "branch and merge hell."

There is a good article in The Hub on Developing On Main/ Trunk Based Development at gro.team/cto-cio-bible-3X/hub/

Developing on main can increase velocity and flow, but it takes discipline and isn't right for every team.

Case Study: Accidently Creating A New £1m Revenue Stream

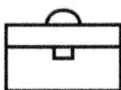

Outcome:

A new £1 million revenue stream was created

Context:

Betfair is an online P2P betting exchange where humans and automated trading engines bet against each other via mobile/web user interfaces and a public API.

Automated trading engines were offering odds on huge numbers of events by "laddering" odds until the value point in the market was reached and the bet was matched. (For example, I'll offer 2 to 1 that Sam Altman will get fired as CEO at OpenAI again. If the bet isn't taken, I'll offer 3 to 1, then 4 to 1, and so on until someone takes the bet and I know where the value point is in the market.

Up to 5 million bets a day were being placed on the Betfair platform and then cancelled without being matched. Betfair's revenue was earned by taking a 2-5% commission on winning bets, so unmatched bets were of zero value to Betfair.

Betfair was suffering from a rapidly growing zero-value transaction volume.

Approach:

I conceived and implemented a transaction charging scheme in which any bet placed on the exchange over a generous threshold would cost 1p a bet through the API or 2p per bet through the website.

It was anticipated that this would disincentivise the odds laddering approach and reduce the amount of zero-revenue transactions being placed on the exchange.

Results:

The automated laddering agents did not, in fact, change their approach. Instead, they paid the transaction charges, thereby creating a brand-new revenue stream for Betfair of more than £1 million per year (which we were OK with!)

Key Lessons Learnt:

- Customer behaviour is hard to predict but always needs to exist within a commercially sustainable commercial framework.

Running A Tech Platform Recap

Effective management of a tech platform includes ensuring operational stability and considering the balance between maintaining current services and innovating for the future.

Staging environments may not always be cost-effective; alternatives like Testing in Production (TIP) can provide real-time insights and are used by leading tech companies.

Managing technical debt is crucial; its "costs" should be made explicit and addressed strategically during planned work to minimise negative impacts on velocity.

Technology team budgets are primarily consumed by personnel and cloud costs; managing these costs proactively and negotiating with suppliers can prevent unexpected expenses.

Developing directly on the main branch can boost productivity for mature teams but requires discipline to avoid integration issues, and innovations can sometimes lead to unexpected but significant new revenue streams.

Running A Tech Team

The broad principles that should apply to running a tech team at maximum efficiency and happiness are:

- Use a modern asynchronous channel-based communication platform like Slack as the primary communication channel
- Minimise the use of Email and WhatsApp, among others, for internal communication
- Use dedicated channels appropriately to minimise the context-switching team members need to do
- Minimise the number of layers in the team; ideally, with no more than 5 layers 1. Engineer 2. Senior 3. Head Of 4. Director/VP 5. CTO
- Keep team sizes small; big teams are slow teams.
- Make sure each team has a common purpose and an unambiguous business reason to exist. If stand-ups don't work because different groups within the stand-up are concerned with different things, then the structure needs changing (see Build And Run below)
- Use Retrospectives, aka Retros, for process innovation. Retros are one of the most effective agile development rituals during which a team gets together every couple of sprints (say every month or so) to write post-it notes of ideas that they stick into "Do More," "Do Less," "Start"

and "Stop" categories. This way, the SDLC/WoW (Way of Working) can be continuously enhanced and improved.

Build And Run

There is no perfect way to cut it, but I like to separate out build and run responsibilities. Some people like to take a "you built it, you support it" approach, but I find it less effective overall in most situations.

I think Separate Build (development) and Run (operational support) teams work better overall because of the following:

1. Each team has a clear and singular focus
2. Estimation and planning are more effective without having to factor in a variable support workload into the SDLC
3. Team members get frustrated if they cannot concentrate on their core responsibilities or miss deadlines due to support work.

The Run Team needs to be managed so that there are good entry and exit points into it with a natural talent conveyor belt and average tenure of 18-24 months. Most team members are happy to "pay their dues" but usually see a role in a core product team as their ultimate destination.

It's a truism, but tech people tend to be more introverted than extroverted. They are generally logical and rational, valuing logical argument and reasoning.

I've had to point out the "etiquette" sometimes when providing pizza or beer for teams and tell people that the point isn't to grab the food/drink and then take it back to their desks. The whole point is that we eat/drink together as a team.

Always go out of your way to give or pass on nice comments to other people. If something nice is said about someone, tell them. If I can't do it immediately, I sometimes write positive comments so I don't forget them. It costs nothing, but positive feedback can mean everything to other people.

Sometimes, it is easy to react angrily in the moment if someone sends an inflammatory email, but never, ever reply angrily. Good discipline is forcing yourself to wait and reply the next day. 99 times out of 100, you will be glad you waited and responded appropriately.

Deadlines

In my experience, the single biggest issue that CEO and CTO CIOs fall out about is deadlines (I know, in other news...bears sh*t in the woods)

CEOs can get very frustrated with missed "deadlines" (which they see as the most important thing). CTO CIOs can adopt positions like "in Agile deadlines don't matter – maximising customer benefit delivery is what matters" and so on.

So, who is right?

As always, the optimum point is somewhere in between deadlines being the most important thing and not mattering at all

At the risk of having my Agile "card" taken off me, my starting point is that deadlines do matter...a lot.

"Deadlines" get factored into business plans and financial models and are essential when coordinating with third parties around PR, launch, marketing, fulfilment, etc.

A high-performing team will take pride in "saying what it does and doing what it says," and hitting it's target dates is a big part of that.

However, if created and used in a binary good/bad way, deadlines can incentivise the wrong behaviors and be a net negative for organisations.

It's true that organisations should be concerned with maximising the benefit delivery to customers and that "arbitrary" or intermediate deadlines can make that slower, not faster.

The nuanced, more pragmatic approach to creating and using deadlines is to:

- Create and communicate the minimum number of "deadlines" needed to manage overall programme third-party and team coordination
- Once created, execution teams will always need to try to find ways to hit their deadlines. If that means postponing (or de-scoping) certain functionality, then that is normally the "least worst" outcome
- If it's an option, delivering early and iterating MVPs is normally a much better way of delivering customer

benefit than "big bang" events and their associated deadlines.

- Go-to-market strategies should be broken down into POC, Prototype, MVP, Soft Launch, Hard Launch, and phases to maximise flexibility and prevent suboptimal outcomes.

In one of the engagements, a lot of conflict and mutual bad feeling between the CEO and delivery teams was created due to using a calendar quarter-centric roadmap. The delivery teams felt that work was being artificially chopped up into quarter-sized chunks that didn't make sense and that their efforts to hit or miss that quarter's deadlines were the only thing ever discussed. The solution to this problem was to remove the quarterly overlay in the plan/roadmap. The deadlines were set for what made sense for the deliverable stream in question, with some projects taking less than a quarter and some taking more. A lot of points of conflict were removed.

Managing High Performers

Hiring 10X Developers

Although some people deny that they exist (like they deny that UFOs and full stack developers exist), "10X" developers do exist, and you want them in your team.

Writing software is a creative process, so some developers can have 10X more business impact than other developers in the same way that some musicians, authors, etc, are 10X more commercially successful than others.

So, how do you find and manage your 10X developers?

The first and most obvious point is that they won't respond to your job postings. You will need to go and find them, and some of the places where you'll find them are as follows:

- Answering questions on Stack Overflow
- Contributing to open-source projects
- Hanging around in Discord channels
- Posting interesting/useful content on Twitter
- Producing video content for YouTube, TikTok, etc.

☛ The ROI in finding and hiring a 10X developer will be positive. They can do things other developers can't do and do things literally 10 times more quickly.

Managing 10X Developers

Great, now you have managed to hire some 10X developers. How do you keep them happy, productive, and impactful?

More so than the rest of us, 10X developers need to be given the opportunity to learn, explore, push boundaries, and try new things. They are best deployed in teams breaking new ground, facing significant challenges, or implementing new technologies or systems.

10X developers tend to focus more on the challenge and opportunity to learn in a role than comp. But in my experience, if you don't reward them in a way commensurate with their higher business impact, then someone else will.

❶ Rewarding high performers monetarily is necessary but not sufficient to keep them happy. High performers tend to value the opportunity to learn and challenge themselves more than comp. If you fail to manage them proactively and appropriately, you will one day get an unwelcome resignation email as they disappear seeking the challenge they have been missing.

The Value Of Stock Options

I firmly believe in the value and benefit of allocating stock options as deep into the team as possible. These schemes can be difficult to set up and manage, but SaaS platforms make it much easier now. Some people can indeed be sceptical about the value of stock options, but that doesn't matter. For the people who do value them, they are very important hiring and retention tools.

Of course, not all work in a team pushes boundaries and breaks new ground, which is why we need a spectrum of talent in a team. Having proportionally too many 10X developers in a team wouldn't be sustainable either.

One of my "golden rules" is to always disagree privately 1:1 face-to-face ideally, and agree/praise publicly 1:many. If you can't discuss a face-to-face disagreement, a video call is the next best thing.

Kaizen Days/Google Time/10%/20% Time

Formally allocating a percentage of team time for "off roadmap" R&D and innovation projects is something that a lot of teams/companies try because they think they should. But most teams/companies are not getting the value they should get from doing it.

❗ Most "20% time" initiatives/schemes don't deliver a positive ROI for the people paying the bills

To get value out of your approach, some things to bear in mind are:

- The benefits of "innovation" time should be twofold: firstly, to create innovative products/services for the company, and secondly, to challenge, develop, and motivate the team
- The art of running innovation schemes is to create a win-win in which developers can self-select the things they do within a framework of potential positive outcomes for the company
- It's a subtle situation; the team members need to feel that they are choosing how to spend the time, but the company needs to feel that they are getting value for money.

☛ One approach that has worked well in teams I have run is inviting the wider team to self-organise into cross-functional project teams to deliver innovative products/services they ideate and suggest themselves. A Dragon's Den/Shark Tank-like pitch event is held where the teams pitch for "investment" into their proposed projects. This works well because it's self-selecting in that the people who want to participate can get involved, but everyone isn't forced to do it. It encourages cross-team collaboration, and the company can shape the outcomes into directions it is happy to invest in. The event at which the teams do their pitches is also always a fun cross-team event.

Running A Tech Team Recap

Running a tech team efficiently requires modern communication tools like Slack, minimizing emails, and using communication channels effectively while keeping team structures flat and teams small to ensure agility.

Differentiating between 'Build' and 'Run' responsibilities can lead to clearer focus and better planning, with a recommended approach to avoid reactive decisions in conflict situations.

Deadlines should be managed pragmatically, balancing the importance of meeting business expectations with delivering customer benefits, and innovating product deployment strategies to avoid rigid deadline pressures.

For managing high performers, especially 10X developers, provide challenges and learning opportunities and ensure compensation reflects their impact, using stock options as an incentive where possible.

Kaizen Days or "20% time" initiatives should have a structured approach to encourage innovation while ensuring company and team members feel the mutual benefits of the investment in off-roadmap projects.

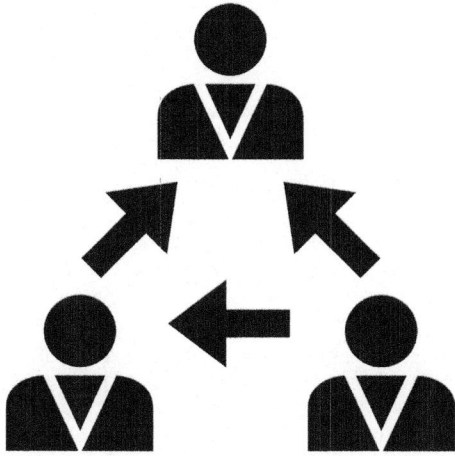

Section 3: Changing A Tech Platform And Team

Changing A Tech Platform

Project Health Check List

Project Objectives and Scope

- Are the project objectives clear and aligned with business goals?
- Is the project scope well-defined and understood by all stakeholders?

Timeline and Schedule

- Is the project on schedule?
- Are there any significant delays, and if so, what are the causes?

Budget and Cost Management

- Is the project within budget?
- Are expenditures being tracked and managed effectively?

Quality of Deliverables

- Are the deliverables meeting the quality standards set for the project?
- Is there a process in place for quality assurance and control?

Team Performance and Resources

- Is the project team adequately staffed and skilled?

- Are team members meeting their performance expectations?
- Is there effective communication and collaboration within the team?

Risk Management

- Have potential risks been identified and assessed?
- Are there plans in place to mitigate identified risks?

Stakeholder Engagement

- Are stakeholders actively engaged and supportive of the project?
- Is there regular and effective communication with stakeholders?

Project Governance and Compliance

- Are the project governance structures working effectively?
- Is the project compliant with relevant regulations and standards?

Change Management

- Is there a process in place to manage changes to the project?
- How are changes affecting the project's scope, schedule, and budget?

Project Documentation and Reporting

- Is project documentation up to date and organised?
- Are project reports accurate and providing a clear picture of project health?

Customer or End-user Satisfaction

- Is there feedback from customers or end-users?
- Are customer needs and expectations being met?
- Lessons Learned and Continuous Improvement
- Are lessons from project experiences being documented and applied?
- Is there a culture of continuous improvement within the project team?

The M O S T framework

If leadership is about one thing, It's change. Hence, we will describe in detail what I call the Mission Objectives Strategy Tactics (or MOST) framework to help you think about, structure, and communicate your change initiatives and agenda.

A manager manages the impact of interruptions and events to try to maintain things as they are. However, a leader identifies the need for and then delivers change.

What might be called Devine's First Law of Leadership is that a team will remain at rest or in a state of uniform motion in a straight line unless acted upon by a leader.

The M O S T framework is a really effective way of going about your leadership business because it forces you to structure your time and focus your energy on the most important things. It also creates clear links between your business strategy and what the tech team is doing this week, this month, and this year...which your CEO will love.

The M.O.S.T. (Mission Objectives Strategies Tactics) Framework

What everyone needs these days of increased competition and volatility is a strategic framework through which to deliver their big-picture business goals whilst improving their capabilities to make tactical execution more impactful and effective.

In other words, we need to create a map showing everyone inside and outside the tech team exactly where we're trying to get to as a team and which paths we should choose today, this week, this month, and this year to get us there most effectively.

👉 Creating a well-communicated strategic framework will also allow you to empower people and teams more effectively. Suppose people genuinely understand where they ultimately need to get to. In that case, they will be much happier making "option a" or "option b" decisions, and you won't need to micromanage them.

❗ The days of five-year strategies are long gone. These days, our strategy needs to make short-term execution more effective and not be somehow separate and different from it.

📖 In his excellent book Winners And How They Succeed, Alastair Campbell talks about OST, an acronym for Objective Strategy and Tactics. If we add an M for Mission to the front of that acronym to make it 'MOST,' I think we have a framework that can really help maximise execution effectiveness.

In M O S T, **'M'** is for Mission. Our **Mission** is the big-picture change we want to achieve.

'O' is for OBJECTIVES. Our objectives are **HOW** we will achieve our Mission. Your objectives should be a mix of direct business results (such as higher revenue and or lower costs) and structural capabilities that will help achieve current and future business goals.

'S' is for STRATEGIES. Our strategy is our big picture **WHAT**. In other words, what will we do to achieve our objectives?

'T' is for TACTICS. Tactics are the 4-10 things we will do **NOW** to execute our strategies.

Mission → How → What → Now might be a helpful way to remember your MOST

The Mission and Objectives are WHATS, but the Strategies and Tactics are HOWS.

It might be helpful when creating your M.O.S.T. to visualise a pyramid with 1 Mission, 2-5 Objectives, 3-6 strategies, and 4-10 Tactics.

Usually, create a M.O.S.T. per full or half financial or calendar year and represent and summarise it on one page broken down into 3-month quarters. That makes it very easy to communicate and iterate.

There is a M.O.S.T. template and sample MOSTs in The Hub at gro.team/cto-cio-bible-3X/hub/

Don't forget to co-create and collaborate when creating your M.O.S.T. The CEO, ExCo, and leaders in your team need to buy into it and feel that they helped create it.

People are much less likely to tear down something that they helped create

Putting the MOST on one page is also very important and necessary. Refine your MOST until you can represent it clearly and succinctly on one page.

Remember that the Strategies and Tactics can and should change any time something material changes in their context.

Changing A Tech Platform And Team Recap

Assess team performance and resources, manage risks proactively, engage stakeholders regularly, and ensure governance and compliance.

Implement a robust change management process, keep accurate and organized documentation and reporting, and prioritize customer or end-user satisfaction.

Foster continuous improvement through lessons learned and maintain a MOST framework (Mission, Objectives, Strategies, Tactics) to link strategy to execution.

The MOST framework helps clarify why change is needed (Mission), what is expected (Objectives), how to achieve it (Strategies), and immediate actions (Tactics), fostering collaboration and ownership among stakeholders.

Mission → What → How → Now might be a good way to remember it.

Section 4:
Our Mission

What Is A Misson?

In this CTO ¦ CIO Bible series, we discuss using a Mission, Objectives, Strategies, and Tactics approach to being a super successful CTO ¦ CIO.

To create our MOST strategic execution framework, we will first need a Mission. The mission should be clear, simple, and compelling. Connecting the dots from the overall company strategy to the Tech Team's mission should be very easy.

Our Mission needs to be a big thing that moves the needle, and It also needs to be clear: simply described and achievable.

A MISSION is the big-picture change we want or need to make to go from where we are now to where we want to be.

Your mission will probably be necessary but insufficient to achieve your company's business plan and must be completely aligned with your company's agenda.

Example Mission themes might be:

- The need for speed (i.e., deliver faster)
- Take the handbrake off (i.e., remove constraints)
- Be the best (i.e., create a competitive advantage for your company)

- Trimming the fat (i.e. save money)
- No stopping until number one (i.e., achieve pre-eminence in your market)

A short, pithy Mission description like this won't be able to encapsulate all of the challenges and complexity your team is facing. But what it can do is clearly describe the single most important thing your team needs to achieve to help your company survive and thrive.

Another way to think about the Mission is if your team was a company or brand, what would you want your strap line to be? What would you like people to think your team is about?

The main challenge my company was facing was making the interest payments on the money borrowed to expand geographically during its glory years. As a tech team, we ran an all-encompassing and nicely branded change initiative that achieved a reduction in the tech team's costs from £55m to £35m a year (primarily with a combination of supplier rationalisation and redundancies). The company survived the crisis and is now a smaller but much more sustainable business.

CEOs love seeing Missions, Objectives, Strategies, and Tactics because they like the concept of making big-picture strategic progress and moving the business forward with impactful near-term delivery. Of course, you only have a limited amount of resources, so focus your efforts where it will affect your customers.

Try to innovate at the customer touch points (web sites, apps, etc.), not way down the stack where your efforts will have little or no effect on customer satisfaction and company success.

So what kind of Objectives should a successful CTO ¦ CIO set, and what are the most important things to focus on?

Section 5:
"How" Objectives

"How" Objectives

Setting objectives for your team is a brilliant opportunity to move the needle in terms of both business results ("What" objectives) and team capabilities ("How" objectives). In fact, top leaders always make sure that they are always working on both of these challenges at the same time.

Objectives should be a mix of both 'What' and 'How' things are. You are unlikely to have the luxury of being able to focus solely on either business results or execution effectiveness; you will need to work on both simultaneously.

Unless you're facing a "burning platform" situation, focusing solely on delivering short-term business results would be a mistake. If you don't concurrently enhance your execution capabilities, you may encounter even greater challenges in the future as the world becomes more competitive and volatile while your execution capabilities remain stagnant.

It would also be a mistake to focus solely on team capability improvements (in some sort of "jam tomorrow" way) building for a future that may or may not ever materialise in the way envisaged. Success is never guaranteed; you need to execute well now to be successful in the future.

A recurring theme in this book is the acknowledgment that we seldom enjoy the luxury of a singular focus. Instead, we often find ourselves serializing tasks, moving from A to B. Given the heightened pace and pressure of the modern world, in many scenarios, it becomes necessary to undertake at least some aspects of both A and B simultaneously rather than opting for an exclusive focus on A or B.

👉 We need business results and capability improvement objectives when setting our objectives. Your company's future success it not a given; it needs to be earned.

👉 Certain CEOs may become frustrated if they perceive the tech team as not contributing to immediate revenue growth. Engaging in discussion with them is crucial, emphasising that enhancing the "what" and the "how" of the tech team is essential for genuine improvement in execution effectiveness. This ensures a comprehensive approach to refining the outcomes and processes, laying the foundation for sustained success.

Think of objectives as the big building blocks you want to create to deliver your mission. They will almost certainly need to be a mix of "what" objectives (direct business or technical improvement) or "how" objectives (improvements in process, technology, or people capabilities).

Of course, if we had to pick, it would make the most sense to start by focusing on our "how" objectives because any improvements we can make in our execution capabilities will only make the achievement of the "what" objectives quicker, better, or cheaper.

As Emanuele Blanco @ Wise says, "The most important thing about being a Tech Leader is making sure you empower your people, set them up for success, and hold them accountable for the results."

Leadership Density

"Leadership" means a lot of different things to different people, but to me, leadership is about one thing: change.

You can assume a leadership role regardless of your current position. Waiting until you reach the C-level is unnecessary. In fact, demonstrating leadership behaviours is often a prerequisite for promotion to the C-level. Therefore, seize opportunities to lead in your current role, as showcasing leadership qualities is a pathway to career advancement.

We should all also aspire to be a leader of leaders. Leadership behaviours should be role-modelled and encouraged at all levels of the team.

In 2008, Google launched an initiative called Project Oxygen to understand common behaviours amongst their highest-performing managers.

Google thinks that the ten things that great leaders do are:

- Coach their people
- Empower their team and avoid micromanaging
- Create a caring team environment
- Be productive and results-oriented
- Be a good communicator

- Discuss development and performance
- Have a clear vision/strategy for the team
- Keep their technical skills up-to-date
- Collaborate across the company
- Be a strong decision maker

In late 2022, OpenAI made a significant entrance with the ChatGPT AI-driven natural language chatbot service, catching attention seemingly out of nowhere. This development prompted Google to declare a "code red," and OpenAI, remarkably, valued itself at $39 billion before generating any revenue. This serves as a powerful reminder not to take the future for granted. Emphasis should be placed on executing well in the present and continually enhancing capabilities to ensure even better execution in the future.

I recommend the book Good to Great: Why Some Companies Make the Leap and Others Don't by James C. Collins as a fascinating analysis of what the companies that step up to greatness have in common. One of the key lessons is "First Who, then What?" or, in other words, get the right people on the bus.

Urgency

Rekindling a sense of urgency has been a recurring team objective in my career. Teams often encounter difficulties when they slip into complacency, introspection, or detachment from the challenges their business is currently facing.

If you think about all of the great people you've worked with in the past, some of the things they probably have in common are that they are passionate about what they do, have energy, and bring urgency.

All great leaders bring urgency into everything they do. They don't set people up for failure (all of their goals are ambitious but achievable). But they want the benefits from the initiative so much that they can't wait to get them and want them NOW.

Malcolm Gladwell thinks that Steve Jobs didn't achieve what he achieved because of intellect or hard work but because of his urgency. "Urgency," Gladwell declared, "characterises Jobs and other immortal entrepreneurs. Jobs is rushed, he's urgent, and that was a part of his genius."

"The difference isn't resources," Gladwell added. "It's ATTITUDE."

One of the start-up CEOs I worked for used to come into work every Monday and manufacture a sense of crisis and high urgency around a carefully chosen single problem or opportunity. We'd all focus on making progress on the issue before Monday, when we knew the cycle would start all over again. By "stirring the pot" like this, the CEO ensured the team was always moving forward with urgency and high focus on what he considered the most important thing.

Ollie Cook (who does SRE @ Apple) says, "The most important thing about being a Tech Leader is admitting when you get something wrong and changing course to correct. Teams will quickly lose patience with and faith in leaders who can't say those simple words."

BUSYNESS spelt with a 'y' IS BAD FOR BUSINESS spelt with an 'I.' Don't make the mistake of confusing busyness with urgency. Urgency is an impatience to achieve business outcomes. It is not the same thing as being busy with activities that may or may not lead to positive business outcomes.

Clarity

Another very important HOW objective is Clarity:

Increased clarity is an objective that will pay dividends across both the team and organisation by enabling faster decision-making and overall execution.

In my experience, I've observed two types of individuals: 1. Those who derive satisfaction from simplifying and clarifying things, and 2. Those who find a certain pleasure in managing complexity and thus may not feel compelled to clarify situations.

Don't succumb to complacency; always make an effort to clarify and simplify situations or problems. Enhancing the clarity of a concept or message not only facilitates smoother communication but also significantly boosts its chances of successful reception.

As Alex Farr (the Group Chief Technology Officer at Christie Group plc) says, "The most important thing about being a technology leader is recognising that you are always learning and always needing to reinvent yourself. We are fortunate in our roles that the continuous evolution of technology along with the changes in working practises and people's needs bring with it excitement and a challenge."

📖 I recommend the book *How to Build a Billion Dollar App* by George Berkowski as a very insightful and comprehensive description of building and launching successful apps. I'm not saying that just because I'm featured in it either (as "Rory" Devine, by the way, George!)

As they mature as a leader, many people go through a stage where they focus on what is best for their team rather than their company. Maybe it's a natural stage of the leadership journey. But it's essential that at the C level, we all see our jobs as co-delivering the company business plan.

High Performance

"Improved Delivery" is a frequently assigned "WHAT" objective that many CEOs aim to instill in their Tech teams. However, defining delivery can be challenging as it encapsulates a multitude of attitudes, behaviors, and impact measures. It serves as an aggregate term, encompassing various factors contributing to the overall effectiveness and success of a team's endeavors.

Every CEO knows when they're not getting as much delivery as they would like, though, and they're not usually shy about voicing their opinion.

👉 I often establish a compact full-stack "Rapid Development" team responsible for delivering weekly drops of tactical fixes and enhancements. I firmly believe in not letting quick and easy tasks get stuck behind larger, more complex ones, as this can lead to considerable stakeholder frustration when seemingly simple issues take a long time to address.

When stakeholders inquire about the feasibility of a task, it's crucial not to convey reluctance. Instead, respond with a positive tone, saying something like, "Let's take a look at it; if it's possible, we'll get it done." Building trust with stakeholders is essential—they need to feel confident that you genuinely want to address their concerns. Once they trust that you would meet their deadlines if it were feasible, they are more likely to believe you if you have to convey that certain things are not possible.

Agility

The Manifesto for Agile Software Development (on the web at agilemanifesto.org) was created in 2001 with four key approaches that we should favour:

One: Individuals and interactions over processes and tools.

Two: Working software over comprehensive documentation.

Three: Customer collaboration over contract negotiation.

Four: Responding to change, over following a plan.

Agile is a How, not a What. There are no prizes for the purest and most orthodox implementation of Agile. If a team isn't focusing on creating working software, it might have fallen into the trap of admiring the process rather than delivering business impact.

Introducing Agile is one of the few truly transformative things you can do for a business. Make sure you use "Retrospective" sessions to ensure that your approach is adaptive and is always improving...

Agile as a noun

Agile development was invented partly because writing a functional specification takes too long and always contains omissions and errors. By the time the functionality is delivered, the real world will have moved on, so what the customer wants and needs will have changed anyway.

It is much better to pilot or prototype and then iterate based on real customer usage rather than to try to predict and plan the future based on imperfect information in a changing world. Early delivery and fast iteration is the route to success...MVP like a boss

Agile doesn't mean "no deadlines," "no documentation," "no interference," or any of the other excuses that Agile zealots use to avoid doing the things they don't want to do. Alarm bells should ring loudly if you hear "pair programming." Whether you like it or not, you may have joined the congregation at a high church of Agile

There is an allegory used in Agile circles about a chicken and a pig to point out the difference between commitment and involvement during daily stand-ups. One day, the chicken decides that the two should start a restaurant. "What should we call it?" says the pig. The chicken thinks and suggests, "Ham and Eggs!" To which the pig replies, "No thanks, I'd be committed. You'd only be involved."

Avoid "drive-by MVPs," whereby a sub-standard version of the product is launched by a team that quickly moves on to the next thing without ever iterating and improving the MVP. Aim for what some people are calling a Minimum Lovable Product.

An MVP should consist of a small "vertical" sub-set of the finished product's features working as well as can be delivered in the time available. It shouldn't be a "horizontal" slice of all of the product's features implemented sub-optimally.

"Agile" principles can also be used very effectively to deliver GROWTH rather than software (covered later).

Simplicity

In addition to the advantages of prioritizing clarity, substantial benefits can be derived from emphasizing simplicity in all aspects of your operations. Businesses can find themselves burdened with excessively intricate technology and process landscapes if they neglect active management of their technology architecture and operating model complexity.

While teams are often eager to build and launch new initiatives, it's relatively rare to witness initiatives focused on the removal of software, systems, or processes. A noteworthy exception occurred at a Fintech company where a legacy Ruby monolith was aptly named "Frankie" (short for

Frankenstein). One of the teams set a key objective to reduce the Lines Of Code (LOC) as a measure of simplification. This example illustrates the potential benefits of actively simplifying and streamlining existing structures for improved efficiency and effectiveness.

Sponsor initiatives to simplify your technology estate and operating model. It's not as glamorous as launching a new product or service. But you will definitely make things quicker, better, or cheaper.

Supplier rationalisation is an often-overlooked way of simplifying and taking cost out of your business. You won't win many fans at the suppliers you rationalise, but the benefits can be material.

If you run a global business with completely incon-sistent and incoherent technology and business oper-ations, then maybe, just maybe, implementing an ERP system without customisation, is a good step forward. Oth-erwise, avoid it like the plague. They can be inflexible and expensive and have brought down many businesses.

Accountability

One of the things that marks out a high performer is their desire to seek out and take accountability for business out-comes. You can't take accountability as a CTO or CIO if you can't also give it.

While there are no one-size-fits-all solutions to improve a team's performance, if there were silver bullets, fostering a culture of accountability would likely be one of them. To enhance accountability, I prefer to distinguish between "Build" and "Run" aspects when structuring teams. This separation ensures a clearer line of accountability for software or service delivery, avoiding dilution of responsibility.

It's essential to clarify that promoting accountability doesn't equate to fostering a blame culture. The objective is to cultivate a sense of personal ownership for business outcomes, not to point fingers when things go awry.

When implementing a culture of accountability, avoid creating structures that assign responsibility without corresponding control. For instance, holding someone accountable for the performance of an external supplier or a separate team can set individuals up for failure. Establishing realistic expectations and providing individuals with the necessary authority ensures that accountability is meaningful and achievable.

📖 *Will It Make the Boat Go Faster?* by Harriet Beveridge and Ben Hunt-Davis is indeed a highly recommended book. Written by an Olympic gold medalist in rowing and an executive coach, the book offers valuable insights into how the strategies employed by Ben Hunt-Davis to achieve Olympic success can be applied to various aspects of business and life.

👉 The response to constructive feedback when telling someone there are performance issues is telling. A performer will ask for more feedback and help turn the situation around. However, an underperformer will say the feedback has negatively affected their morale.

Shared Goals

Once you have created your mission, you need to ask yourself honestly whether your team is willing and able to share the new goals implied?

For disruptive missions that necessitate a change in a company or team's business or operating model, it is by no means a given that your team will agree with the need for fundamental change.

☞ We really are creatures of habit. People fundamentally don't like change, which is why delivering change initiatives is hard and liable to failure.

Sometimes, resistance will be active (with people openly disagreeing). But it will often be passive, with people just not engaging with the change activities.

Getting the right people on the bus may necessitate exiting people unwilling or unable to contribute to the mission. As human beings, this is always the most difficult and unpleasant part of leadership. But we always need to remember in these situations that what we're doing is best for most people and may make the difference between survival and failure for a company and its employees.

❗ I once had to make a valued employee redundant, and his pregnant wife, who was a teacher, collapsed in front of her class when he called to share the news. It was awful to have to do, but the tough measures we took did save the company (and hundreds of jobs). In fact, the company survived and went on to IPO very successfully.

As Rich Phillips (a technology leader CTO/CIO with substantial media technology experience & expertise) says, "The most important thing about being a Tech leader is not the technology. It's building teams of diverse talent, giving them a purpose that they can be passionate about and empowering them to deliver - while guiding and supporting them to fulfil their potential to the benefit of the business."

Case Study: Stopping Envelopes And Saving The Planet

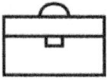

Outcome:

1.5 million envelopes per year were prevented from being sent

Context:

I was at a media business facing disruption from digital products and services. The Head of Operations informed me that customers purchasing our new service package were receiving up to fifteen confirmation letters by post due to the limitations of the legacy ERP system.

Although it wasn't directly under my responsibility as CTO, I assigned Mark Parsonage to lead a project with a straightforward scope: "Stop the envelopes."

Throughout the project, my key contribution was consistently saying, "No—just stop the envelopes!" every time a team attempted to derail or delay the project by suggesting the need for new tools, teams, processes, or other additions.

Approach:

I picked Mark, a team member with high personal effectiveness and agency, to deliver an "off-piste" project with high impact, importance, and urgency.

Results:

The project successfully achieved its goal. At the time, it was calculated that we prevented the sending of 1.5 million envelopes per year, resulting in substantial benefits for customer satisfaction, cost savings, and the environment.

Key Lessons Learnt:

- Don't stand behind a counter flipping burgers and waiting for orders. Do whatever you can to help your business.
- Great people like Mark Parsonage are capable of doing great things, given the opportunity and unwavering backing.

Competitive Advantage

The most effective way to make your business successful is to give it a competitive advantage. If a business has a competitive advantage, it can do things other businesses can't do, or it can do the things other businesses can do "quicker, better, or cheaper."

To create a competitive advantage, you and your team need to do something better than all of the competitor's teams in your industry. Therefore, creating a competitive advantage is easy to say but not so easy to do.

When I was at Betfair, we were matching online transactions at such low latency (sub 20 milliseconds) that a delegation from the London Stock Exchange visited us to ask us how we were doing it.

As Dave Roberts (a global IT Director | Non-Executive Director | Tech Mentor | Podcast Host | BCS Chartered Fellow) says, "The most important thing about being a Tech Leader is to ensure that you make room for innovation. Create a space that allows people to innovate and try new ideas and deliver organisational value rapidly in an iterative manner."

"High output management" by Andrew Grove is full of great advice from the former CEO of Intel about how to build and run a company as a set of repeatable production processes. As Andy puts it, "Manage short-term objectives based on long-term plans."

Does that sound familiar?

The meaning of competitive advantage for your business is entirely contextual. However, strategies typically conceived to create a competitive advantage often include:

- Launch a unique product or service- A
- Integrate previously disconnected things- B and C
- Apply technique into a new area- D
- Do things quicker, better, or cheaper- E

Never underestimate the power of making things easier, quicker, or cheaper for your customers.

Reminder: as a CTO CIO, you need to keep an eye on all emerging technology capabilities for opportunities to use them to create a competitive advantage for your company.

One route to competitive advantage is gaining actionable insight from data. I have embedded a data scientist within all of the scrum teams at a number of companies.

At Hailo, the "Driver" Team found a number of creative ways to increase the Driver Acceptance Rate by deriving actionable insight from data.

One seemingly straightforward aspect that often creates challenges for teams is establishing a clear and universally understood "Definition of Done" (DoD). Different team members may interpret " Done" differently, leading to potential misunderstandings. For example, a developer might perceive a task as complete once the coding is finished. At the same time, a Scrum Master may insist on considering it done only after coding, testing, and release to customers. It's crucial to reach a consensus and communicate what makes the most sense within your specific context. In my experience, defining something as done only when customers actively use it tends to minimise confusion.

"How" Objectives Recap

Set "What" and "How" objectives for your team, focusing on immediate business results and capability improvements to ensure future success.

Leadership should be demonstrated at all levels, encouraging behaviours like coaching, communication, and strong decision-making to drive change.

Urgency in execution is crucial; foster a culture where deadlines are respected, and every team member strives for immediate and impactful results.

Maintain clarity and simplicity across projects to enhance understanding and decision-making while driving team accountability.

Balance innovation with operational excellence, using Agile methodologies to deliver growth and ensure competitive advantage by empowering teams to iterate and improve rapidly.

Section 6:
"What" Objectives

"What" Objectives

So far, we have covered a lot of very important "HOW" objectives, such as agility, simplicity, accountability, and so on, but what about some "WHAT" objectives?

Defining "WHAT" objectives is inherently context-dependent and specific to the unique circumstances of a business. It's crucial to avoid approaching it with a mindset of "this is the solution; now tell me about the problem."

The sort of thing that normally gets created as a "WHAT" objective is as follows:

- Expand into country A or market B
- Retire or replace system C
- Launch new product or service D
- Acquire company or team E

☞ When planning or delivering new functionality, it's crucial to emphasize the benefits rather than getting distracted by the features. While the "How" is important, maintaining a focus on the "What" – the customer benefits you aim to deliver – is key. As Theodore Levitt aptly put it, "Sell the Hole, Not the Drill."

❗ It's critical to pick important and impactful "WHAT" objectives, ideally directly drawn from the business plan.

Leadership is about change, and it's your job at the C level to identify the opportunities for improvement in your business, turn them into objectives, and lead the change to achieve them.

Looking at some of these common "What" objectives in the abstract...

Expansion Into New Markets

The broad principles that apply when expanding into new territories or markets are the following:

- Maximise the amount of work you avoid. In other words, leverage your existing infrastructure and operating model as much as possible. Only embark on new initiatives or tasks when absolutely necessary.
- Customise new technology or workflows as little as possible. If customisation is essential (like supporting a new language), push it out to the edge as much as possible. Protect your core systems from customisation as much as possible.
- Consider white-labeling or rebranding an existing product or service in the new market for the initial year or two. This approach allows you to test and learn about the best value proposition and product-market fit in the new market. If the launch into the new market doesn't prove successful for any reason (as many don't), you've minimised the extent of work and changes made.
- Maintaining a loose coupling to the core systems and operating models may be the optimal approach in new markets. On the flip side, failure could result from not

customizing or adapting your product/service enough to succeed in the new market. It's crucial to evaluate the costs and benefits on a case-by-case basis.

- Don't overlook the potential for high opportunity costs when entering new markets. It's essential to assess whether the new opportunity is genuinely significant enough to warrant effectively deprioritizing work on the core value proposition that has been driving your current success.

Replatforming And Replacement

- It's worth reiterating the initial point: maximize the amount of work you avoid. Only retire or replace systems if the constraints they impose are significant or fundamental to your operations.

- Has the business case cost/benefit of the move been done properly? The cost of change of replacing legacy systems can be very high.

- If you're not in a "burning platform" situation, don't "big bang" any changes. Put an API in front of the legacy system and gradually manage and shape the traffic/ work away from the legacy system to the new system.

We took this approach when re-platforming from the legacy platforms to Hailo 2.0 or H2O. We put an API in front of the legacy platforms. We then gradually increased traffic to the new platforms from 0 to 100% as the functionality and scalability were created in H2O. Overall, the approach worked very well.

Product Launches

Whole books are written on managing product development/launches, but some of my "lessons learnt" are as follows:

- Ensure early delivery and iterate on an MVP. Avoid attempting to plan, predict, or achieve perfection, as none of us possess the perfect information required for such feasibility.

- Ensure end-to-end testing is conducted as early as possible in the project, preferably after a few sprints. Typically, end-to-end testing is scheduled towards the project's end, and if issues arise, there might not be sufficient time to address them without causing commercial damage and potential embarrassment due to date or scope shifts.

☞ A significant number of project delays I've observed in my career could likely have been mitigated with early and effective end-to-end (E2E) testing. Connecting the Minimum Viable Products (MVPs) early on ensures that everything is functioning as expected sooner rather than later. If this testing involves users or customers, all the better. Refer to The Biggest Mistakes Of My Career for additional insights.

Amazon's "Start with a Press Release" Approach

Amazon's "start with a press release" approach is a unique product development and project planning strategy.

Its core principles are:

- Begin with the End in Mind: The core idea is to start the development process by writing a mock press release announcing the finished product. This is done before any development begins.

- Customer-Centric Focus: The press release is written from the customer's perspective and outlines the product's benefits and features as they would be experienced by the customer. This helps ensure the product is designed with the customer's needs and desires at the forefront.

- Clarification of the Idea: Writing the press release forces the team to clarify their ideas and distil the product's value proposition. It must clearly answer why the product is valuable, who it is for, and how it differs from existing products.

- Identification of Key Features: The process helps identify and focus on the key features that will make the product unique and desirable to customers.

- Revision and Iteration: The press release is revised continuously throughout the development process. This iteration ensures the product stays true to the original vision and customer needs.

- Internal Communication Tool: The press release also acts as an internal communication tool, helping to align the development team and other stakeholders around a shared vision.

- Assessment of Market Viability: By envisioning the final product in a real-world context, the team can better assess its market viability and potential challenges.

This approach is part of Amazon's broader philosophy of being customer-obsessed and working backwards from customer needs. It encourages innovative thinking, clear communication, and a strong focus on end-user benefits, which are crucial in developing successful products.

Company/Team Acquisition

Company/team acquisition can be a graveyard for ambition, and I remember seeing a statistic along the lines of "80% of acquisitions fail to deliver the promised business benefits."

So, how should you attack a company/team merger?

- Reiterating the point once more: maximize the amount of work you avoid. Only consider changing something if there are direct top or bottom-line business benefits. Nominal standardisation is often insufficient unless the benefits can be measured in tangible cash terms rather than merely being able to "paint a picture" on a Power-Point presentation.

- The most successful M&A transactions I've observed often involve a gradual convergence between businesses. While some may attempt a "big bang" approach, it's usually to realise cost savings outlined in the merger business case rather than for purer or more strategic reasons, based on my experience.

Acquiring growth through acquisition is often perceived as easier than achieving organic growth.

Leading internal change and improvements can be challenging, especially in cases where M&A is executed with "paper" equity rather than actual funds.

> Don't forget that there are sample MOST templates and objectives at gro.team/cto-cio-bible-3X/hub/

"What" Objectives Recap

"What" objectives should focus on impactful business results and must be context-specific, aiming to advance business goals alongside "How" objectives that enhance team capabilities.

When expanding into new markets, leverage existing infrastructure and minimise customisations to reduce workloads; prioritise impactful objectives directly from the business plan and lead the changes needed.

For replatforming, utilise APIs to transition traffic gradually from legacy systems to new platforms, reducing risk and disruption.

During product launches, focus on early MVP delivery and thorough end-to-end testing to ensure product readiness and customer alignment, using Amazon's "Start with a Press Release" strategy for clear, customer-focused development.

With company or team acquisitions, a gradual convergence is recommended over "big bang" integration, focusing on tangible business benefits rather than standardisation for nominal benefits.

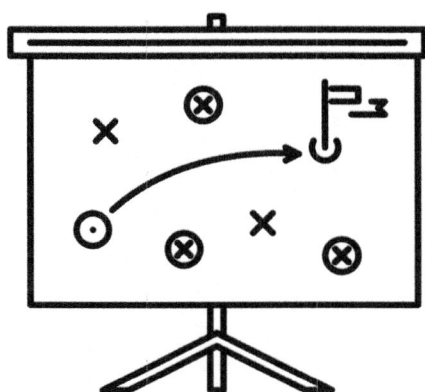

Section 7: Strategies

Strategies

Strategies need to be living, breathing, evolving things. They are not fixed plans carved in stone and only dusted off occasionally. Having an out-of-date strategy is worse than having no strategy because it occupies the space where an effective strategy should be.

You may need to deploy a dual-track or bi-modal strategy to achieve all of your objectives. One side of your strategy could be to pay back technical debt in parallel with the other side of the strategy innovating via a "game changer" (which we will cover later)

The IT strategy needs to be presented alongside the business strategy. The IT strategy informs and is informed by the business strategy. They should be two sides of the same coin.

Focus on Business Success

Some people would argue that the primary role of a CTO ¦ CIO is to use technology to make their company successful. I think there is a lot of truth in that, but let's not forget that all technology leaders (post-early-stage start-ups) execute through people, not technology, at the end of the day.

Emphasizing business success is paramount. Throughout this book, a recurring theme underscores that exceptional CTOs and CIOs maintain a relentless focus on business value and outcomes in all their endeavors.

Certain CTOs and CIOs err by concentrating on input or internal metrics, such as deployment frequency, rather than prioritizing the metrics that truly matter—namely, revenue, profit, costs, productivity, and so forth.

📖 I recommend the book *Think, Do, Show: The Agile 2.0 Secrets to Building Software People Love to Use* by Simon Edwards as a brilliant guide to running high-performance agile teams from a world-class guy who knows what he is talking about.

Measure, Act, Measure

A highly effective strategy for aligning your team with new missions and objectives is to shift the metrics and Key Performance Indicators (KPIs) to ones that specifically target the new goals. In many cases, this adjustment is essential for achieving success.

However, it's crucial to be cautious about unintended consequences. Selecting effective metrics and key results is a combination of art and science. Often, metrics aimed at reducing churn or enhancing conversion are underutilized, making an exploration into these areas a generally wise initiative.

📖 I recommend *From Worst to First: Behind the Scenes of Continental's Remarkable Comeback* by Gordon Bethune as an anecdote-heavy and refreshingly straightforward description of how Continental was turned around.

When leading change, don't overlook the "classic" success metrics such as Customer Satisfaction, Employee Engagement, Net Promoter Score, Time to Market, Return on Investment, etc.

Exercise extreme caution when selecting metrics, as they strongly influence behaviors. An illustrative case involves the influx of emails from LinkedIn, which, after Microsoft's acquisition of LinkedIn, was potentially linked to the compensation scheme of Microsoft's CEO, Satya Nadella, and his C-suite. Their compensation reportedly included a metric based on the "number of times logged-in members visit LinkedIn, separated by 30 minutes of inactivity." What may have been beneficial for the Microsoft CEO's compensation was evidently not aligned with the best interests of LinkedIn's customers.

I also recommend the book Freakonomics by Steven D. Levitt and Stephen J. Dubner as a fascinating look at the difference between causation and connectivity and why drug dealers live with their mothers.

Measuring the efficiency and effectiveness of software development objectively poses challenges due to the creative and design-driven nature of the process. Up to 80% of the effort in producing quality software is often concentrated in the design phase, a dimension that proves challenging to analyze quantitatively.

In my interim engagements, I commonly engage in discussions with the CEO about development metrics. CEOs often feel they aren't receiving sufficient delivery and may aim to substantiate their concerns using metrics like Scrum story points per sprint. However, accurately gauging the intricacies of software development goes beyond these quantitative metrics and requires a nuanced understanding of the creative and design aspects involved.

❗ The disappointing truth is that due to the wide variety in how story points are measured and used by each team, these metrics are only really useful for tracking the trajectory and progress of individual teams using the same Story points approach. Story points are pretty meaningless when comparing across teams.

Some CEOs eventually understand the difficulties in trying to boil down a creative process like software development onto a spreadsheet. But others never really lose their suspicion that there is some sort of tech conspiracy to help tech teams hide under-performance and avoid objective scrutiny.

❝ As Ian Woosey (who is a group CIO, CDO, COO, and Board Advisor) says, "The most interesting thing about being a Tech Leader is there has never been a better time to deliver real and rapid business change through the delivery of innovative technology that really works. That is what every CIO should strive for given the tools available in a digital world."

Rethink Your What, How & When

Avoid the error of treating a "How" as a "What." The programming language you choose for your software is a

"How." Conversely, your website visitor-to-user conversion rate is a "What."

Spend as much time as possible working on the "What," not the "How." Try to do things that directly affect the "What" rather than the "How," which, at best, will have a second-order effect on the "What."

Try to give your team problems (such as improving X by Y%) rather than features to implement. As General Patton said, "Never tell people how to do things. Tell them what to do, and they will surprise you with their ingenuity..."

A team needs to be at the right maturity level before being asked to solve problems rather than deliver features. Doing this with an underperforming or immature team would set them (and your company) up for failure. Their lack of experience and business knowledge will likely result in them delivering sub-optimum solutions.

Perfect Is The Enemy Of Good

I've worked for a few "perfectionists" in my time, and it has always been a struggle. The irony is that perfectionism tends to go hand in hand with arrogance. So perfectionists think they're somehow better than the rest of us who are happy to be pragmatic, compromise, and work below the lofty standards the perfectionist thinks we should all aspire to.

A perfectionist tends to slow down customer benefit delivery by diverting people and teams to focus on relatively unimportant details.

In dealing with perfectionists, as with other negative leadership behaviors discussed in this book, I've found that engaging in factual, constructive, and honest conversations with them is the most effective approach. Pointing out the direct negative consequences of their perfectionist tendencies is usually sufficient to encourage them to mitigate their behaviors. This, in turn, helps minimize the impact of their behavior on the team or project. Consider reviewing your approach to product development in light of these insights.

Flow efficiency and sprint boundaries are a couple of things to monitor when managing classic 2-week scrum development. Flow efficiency refers to the efficiency with which work items move through the different stages of the development process. Sprint boundaries refer to the start and end of sprints in Scrum. It's essential to regularly review and adapt processes to ensure flow efficiency and the effective use of sprint boundaries.

An alternative to the classic two-week sprint Scrum agile is to use a more "Kanban" weekly rhythm where time-boxed development is dropped, estimation is optional (and normally dropped completely), and velocity metrics are replaced by cycle time.

Kanban software development is particularly well-suited to agile development environments, where teams must respond quickly to changing customer needs and market conditions. It emphasizes flexibility, collaboration, and continuous improvement and can help teams to deliver high-quality software more efficiently and effectively.

In Kanban software development, the work is visualised on a board, typically divided into columns representing different stages of the development process. The columns may include stages such as "to do," "in progress," and "done." Tasks or user stories are represented by cards, which are moved from one column to the next as they progress through the development process.

The goal of Kanban software development is to create a smooth, continuous flow of work through the development process, focusing on minimising waste and maximising value for customers. This is achieved by limiting the work in progress at any given time and continuously improving the development process through feedback and collaboration.

I have seen 20-50% improvements in team velocity when switching to a more Kanban approach. It minimises the overheads in a software development life cycle with relatively small and less complex tasks.

Benchmark Your Team's Maturity

Early on your change journey, benchmarking is a great way to get a feel for the stage your team has reached and what capabilities you have or need to build to deliver your Mission and Objectives.

A Capability Maturity Model Is a great lens to evaluate a team through, and the levels most commonly recognised are:

- Level 1: Initial: chaotic, ad hoc, individual heroics. The starting point for the use of a new or undocumented software development life cycle.
- Level 2: Repeatable: the Software Development Life Cycle is documented sufficiently such that repeating the same steps may be attempted.
- Level 3: Defined: the SDLC is defined and managed as a standard business process.
- Level 4: Managed: the SDLC is quantitatively measured in accordance with agreed-upon metrics.
- Level 5: Optimising: Adaptive optimisation and improvement are in place.
- Once you have benchmarked your team, you'll have a much better idea of the WHAT objectives the team might be capable of delivering and the HOW Objectives you might need to build via your strategies.

A book I recommend is *Fish!: A remarkable way to boost morale and improve results* by Stephen C. Lundin, Harry Paul, and John Christensen. In this book, a fish market is studied to show how to bring energy, passion, and a positive attitude to your job every day.

Evaluate And Optimise The Team Structures

The founder of Amazon (Jeff Bezos) believes that no matter how large your company gets, individual teams should never be larger than can be fed with two pizzas.

The number of relationships to be managed in a team of n grows as n squared (n x n) as n grows, so there is a scientific basis to the hypothesis that a set of small co-located teams is the optimum way to organise a large group of people.

My team grew from 35 to 350 at Betfair, and almost as an academic exercise, I used to try to analyse and model whether we were getting 10 times more delivery after a 10X increase in overall team size. As we grew, I got the feeling that we were hitting diminishing returns in terms of the increased value of new hires, and it felt like the teams were getting too big. I rearranged the structure into a set of smaller teams, improving velocity and overall delivery.

A lot of the agile development approaches (stand-ups, scrum boards, etc.) assume sets of 8-10-person independent self-organised teams.

Early in your change journey, you should evaluate how your team is organised to ensure it is optimum for the mission you want the team to deliver.

In general, you should look to:

· Minimise the number of layers in the team; it's advisable to avoid having more than five, counting from the most junior person in the team to the CTO or CIO.

· Minimise the number of roles that don't deliver direct business impact. Tech leads should be a hybrid technical/managerial role, for instance.

· Sets of small independent self-organised teams are generally optimum; small is beautiful.

- Each team should have a common purpose and focus to be effective. Asking a team to be responsible for more than one area (or thing) only dilutes accountability and delivery.

- Shared services or horizontal teams can be more efficient but will be less effective.

☞ Evaluate whether you want to solve for efficiency or effectiveness. If your mission is to "trim the fat" to save money, a central team of data scientists working with delivery teams as needed will be more efficient and cheaper. If your mission is to launch ground-breaking products and services, embedding a data scientist full-time in each delivery team will be more effective (but expensive).

❗ Shared services can easily become shared constraints if the impacts and costs/benefits are not actively managed.

🏛 One of my teams at Hailo was consistently underperforming, and I was struggling to figure out why. Despite having seemingly great individuals who were co-located and following rituals similar to those of the high-performing teams, something was amiss. Then, it struck me — the team lacked diversity, with members sharing the same age, sex, and background. I decided to introduce a different type of person into the team, and the more diversified talent mix had a truly transformative effect on the team's delivery. This experience underscored the invaluable impact of diversity on team dynamics and performance.

Teams should include members with diverse backgrounds and approaches. You should do this not to tick any boxes but because it genuinely improves performance.

Individuals will need to be managed differently. Some people will need a metaphorical "reality check" and challenge to do better. Others will need a metaphorical "arm around their shoulders" and words to build them up. Get to know your people and what motivates and helps them.

People are motivated by different things. In one of my teams, it was very important to one of the most talented developers that he was the highest-paid developer on the team. Once I told him that he was the highest-paid team member, he was happy; his comp in absolute terms didn't bother him.

Don't force great technologists to be poor people managers so that they can achieve more status and reward.

Create two ladders of equivalent roles and job titles in the tech team—something like this.

Technical Ladder

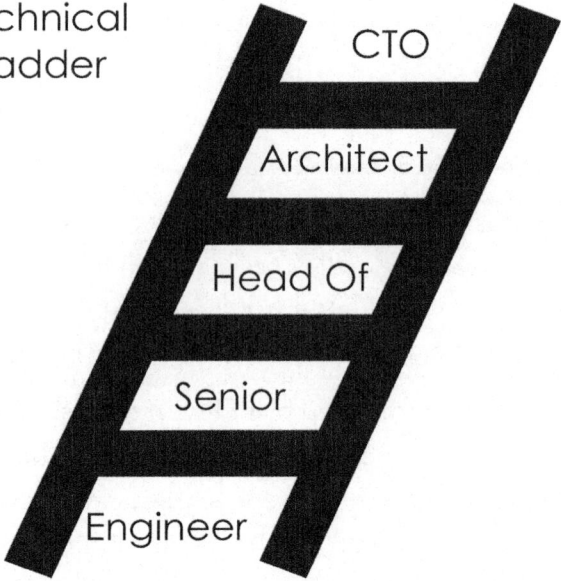

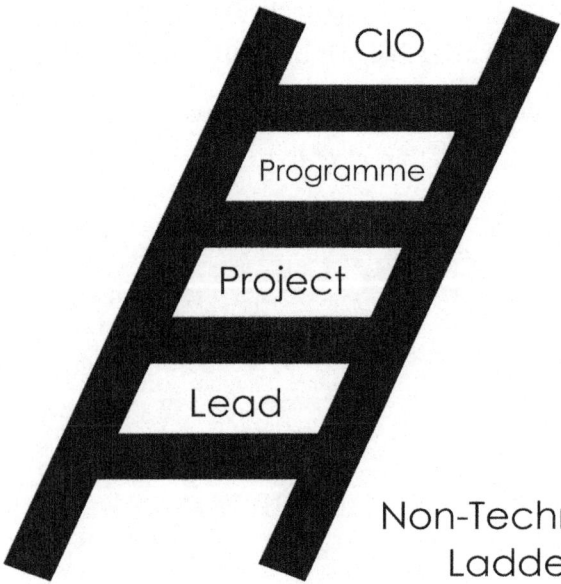

CTO
Architect
Head Of
Senior
Engineer

CIO
Programme
Project
Lead

Non-Technical Ladder

If there is mutual suspicion and sniping between two teams, mix them up and co-locate them. I have done it at a number of companies, and it normally resolves the "us and them" very quickly.

Your Direct Reports Team

Your direct reports (DR) team must have a wide spectrum of experiences and attitudes. You need your ideas and decisions to be constructively challenged in your DR meeting, and that won't happen if there is homogeneity and groupthink.

Your "DR" Dressing Room

I like to make the analogy with my DR Team that our DR meetings should be like half-time during a sports team match. We close the door and talk honestly about what is going well or badly and what we will need to do to win the game. We have total candour and disagree robustly and freely. Once we have discussed the issues, we agree on what we'll do, open the door, and then go back on to the "pitch" as a united team to execute the game plan we have all just agreed to.

Strategies Recap

Strategies must be adaptive and aligned with business goals. A bimodal approach may be necessary to balance paying back technical debt and pursuing innovative projects.

Focus on business outcomes and success, use technology to drive the company forward, and ensure that IT strategies complement and are integral to the overall business strategy.

Metrics should be updated to reflect new missions and objectives, focusing on business impact over internal metrics and avoiding unintended consequences by selecting effective KPIs.

Re-evaluate product development approaches, considering alternatives like Kanban to improve flow efficiency and cycle time and ensure team structures are optimized for mission delivery.

Encourage team diversity to improve performance, manage individuals according to their needs, and ensure that leadership teams challenge constructively to avoid groupthink.

Now that we've established our mission, defined our objectives, and outlined our strategies, the next crucial step is determining our starting point. How do we initiate and propel ourselves forward?

What specific initiatives and tactics should we prioritize to swiftly achieve our objectives and fulfill our mission?

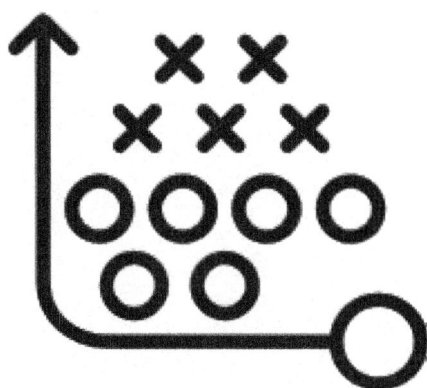

Section 8: Tactics

Tactics

To implement your strategies, you need to carefully choose 5-10 (and only 5-10) tactics per quarter.

Make sure that your tactics are self-describing things you will actually do. For instance, "Improve SEO effectiveness" is a strategy, but "Achieve 10 new high domain authority back links" is a tactic.

Ideally, your tactics need to have a mix of cycle times from one day to three months. We can always add new tactics as our tactics get delivered.

Cycle time is arguably the most useful agile software development KPI/metric. It is defined as a measure of the time it takes to complete a single task from start to finish. It is often used in manufacturing and production environments to assess the efficiency of production processes and identify opportunities for improvement. To achieve low cycle times, a team will need to do a lot of things well.

Don't pick too many tactics, thinking that will somehow make success more likely. Every tactic added reduces the relative weight of all of the other tactics: time and money are normally constrained resources, so prioritise very carefully.

As Steve Homan (the CTO at Instant) says, "The most important thing about being a Tech Leader is to set a path, empower your team then communicate, communicate, communicate and listen, listen, listen. Be clear and be curious."

Balance Results And Relationships

In general, picking the right balance between results and relationship-focused at any time is hugely important. The need for both approaches will vary in time and across roles as well, of course.

Unless you are on a "burning platform," it would be a mistake to drive through your change agenda, leaving a trail of broken relationships and collateral damage in your wake. You will need to create and leverage a network of change agents across the whole company to successfully deliver your Mission, so work with people, not against them.

The CFO at one of my interim engagements once accused me of being brought in to deliver the CEO's agenda "at all costs." He obviously felt that we were getting the Results v Relationship balance wrong, so I made a conscious effort to make sure he felt that we were working with him (and not against him) much more going forward.

The Product and Tech Relationship

I sometimes describe the relationship between Product and Tech (half) jokingly as a loveless marriage. There needs to be healthy tension and mutual respect in this relationship as the "What" and "How" sides of the delivery coin "push and pull" each other to maximise business impact.

INSPIRED: How to Create Tech Products Customers Love by Marty Cagan is a master class in structuring and staffing a vibrant and successful product organisation. One of Marty's insights is that to create great products, we should focus on misery, not technology. Great products fill great needs.

The CPO Role

I have worked with some great (and some awful) Chief Product Owners in my time. The terrible ones take the credit for everything that goes well and blame tech for anything that doesn't go well. But the great ones know that part of their role is actually to help protect the tech team.

Hiring a great CPO like Jon Moore of (Silicon Valley Product Group, IPO'd Trainline) can make a massive difference to a business. In fact, I'd even go so far as to say that the role is nearly as important as CTO (ahem).

You call a lot about a company from their CPO. A great CPO normally means it's a great company.

Choosing How You Fail As A CPO In Founder Driven Company

I sometimes think that the role of CPO in a founder-driven company is the hardest role in modern business. Most founders don't have the technical chops to micro-manage the CTO, but that isn't the case for the CPO. Founders usually have a strong vision for the product, of course, so the CPO can implement the founder's vision without conflict and eventually get fired for being expensive overhead (and "not adding enough value"), or they can try to put their stamp on the product, conflict with the founder and eventually get fired for "not sharing the vision."

I recommend the book *Steve Jobs* by Walter Isaacson as a brilliant look at what made Steve Jobs tick. Steve Jobs said," The way we're running the company, the product design, the advertising, it all comes down to this: Let's make it simple. Really simple..."

The CTO CIO Relationship With the CEO

By a country mile, the most important relationship a CTO | CIO has to manage is with his | her line manager, which is normally the CEO. It's critical that the CTO | CIO is seen to understand, support, and deliver on the CEO's agenda.

The CTO CIO has the most to lose if the relationship with their boss breaks down, so it is very much the CTO CIO's job to proactively manage this relationship. The CEO doesn't have time to think, "What good work did the CTO CIO do this week?" So make it easy for the CEO by telling them at least once a week about all the good work you and your team are doing. Why not copy them on your weekly "Ramblings" missive (covered later)?

A CEO once turned around to me as the CTO in April and said, "I've told the board that we're setting up an offshore development operation in November, so we need to do it." Gulp, I was thinking before he finished off with, "Otherwise, you're fired." Let's just say I thought he was getting the Results v Relationship balance wrong.

As Jack Hollocks (a Technology Consulting Manager at Stott & May Consulting) says, "Enjoy the journey, don't just focus on the end goal. If you are just focusing on reaching go live, producing an MVP or getting funding, it will be a long and tiring journey. Surround yourself with a team that loves the journey and the process of getting there. This is how you get true satisfaction from your work and better results because of it."

Don't Neglect The Basics

As mentioned many times in this book, in any CTO ¦ CIO role, there are usually core product or service delivery responsibilities alongside the product or service development responsibilities. Don't make the mistake of neglecting your product or service delivery responsibilities in favour of your product or service development responsibilities.

There is nothing more important than delivering a great experience to your customers. You literally don't have a business without them. Your product or service must always be available, quick and easy to use. If your app/website is unusable or down, your shop is shut, and shutting up shop is never a good thing for a business.

Ensuring a consistently excellent customer experience involves effective customer demand/load forecasting. It's essential to meticulously plan the software and hardware capacity required to service this demand, ensuring optimal availability and latency.

At Betfair, load forecasting was easy. The load broadly doubled every year over the nearly 5 years I was there.

We created what is now called an SRE Site Reliability Engineering Team that did a great job of ensuring we always had the capacity we needed for high-profile sporting events as traffic grew.

One approach I've seen to work well is using web user experience analysis software like Mouseflow to help the customer service team understand the customer experience they are supporting. Making journeys and heatmaps available to them really helps being the customer experience to life for them.

Internal Customers

A potential mistake is to neglect the needs of your internal customer colleagues. Their tools and systems must also be available, quick, and easy to use at all times.

Authentically caring about the usability and effectiveness of internal tools and systems will win you a lot of friends in your organisation. Many tech leaders make the mistake of ignoring internal stakeholders because they are not as important as real customers. But as always, things aren't that binary. You need to do a great job for both sets of customers. Helping improve other teams' tools and systems will also help you gain supportive stakeholders for your big-picture change journey.

Getting your operational service delivery responsibilities right gets you your seat at the high table. Don't even think about engaging people in forward-looking conversations if you're not delivering the best possible internal and external customer experiences today.

As usual, we won't have the luxury of singular focus. You will need to do the right thing and do the thing right.

Listening

Undoubtedly, your team and company comprise talented individuals. If that's not the case, it becomes your foremost challenge. Collectively, your team likely possesses valuable insights and innovative solutions for the challenges they encounter. Listening to their ideas is key.

At Betfair, we faced low conversion rates due to the complexity of our ten-level deep menu structure. A breakthrough came when one of our engineers suggested placing a search box on the front page—an unconventional move at the time. Embracing this idea led to a remarkable 30% increase in revenue on the day of its launch.

As Executive Leader & CEO John Eikenberry says, "The most wonderful thing about being a Tech Leader is helping to guide a team to grow its ability to take on ever more challenging projects... and watch their joy when they succeed on something they thought was near impossible".

Don't make the mistake of joining a team or organisation with preconceived ideas and things that you want to implement. Spend the first week in a new role listening and understanding the context before starting to offer solutions.

Never join an organisation saying, "Here is your solution. Now tell me about your problem..."

📖 I also recommend the book Accelerate: The Science of Lean Software and Dev Ops: Building and Scaling High Performing Technology Organizations by Nicole Forsgren and Jez Humble. It is a detailed and clear discussion of best practices in building, deploying, and running software.

Be very discriminating about whom you take advice from. There are millions of smart people in the world who could probably provide a credible description of how they would/could solve a particular challenge or problem. But life is a great teacher; in my experience, it pays to work with people who have genuinely "been there and done it."

Professionalism

Call me old-fashioned, but business may have become less formal over the years. There is no need for standards of professionalism to slide.

Professionalism at work can be defined as behaving in a reliable, considerate, respectful, and collaborative way in the physical or virtual workplace.

Professionalism can also be thought of as being a considerable corporate citizen. The more professional you are, the easier you are to work with.

Professional meeting behaviour might be to:

- Turn up on time
- Arrive having done any actions assigned to you
- Demonstrate your concern for the important issues facing the business

- Proactively offer to help solve problems
- Don't surprise or undermine any of the other people in the meeting
- Stay present in the meeting; do not start using your phone or emails.
- Make notes using a laptop, not paper (so you can easily reuse, share, and search the text). Taking notes also has the added benefit of forcing you into active listening mode.

Active listening is a communication technique that involves fully concentrating on and engaging with the speaker to understand their message. It involves giving the speaker your full attention, focusing on their words, body language, and tone of voice. Active listening also requires responding to the speaker to show that you understand and appreciate their message and clarifying any misunderstandings or uncertainties.

I attribute part of my success (ahem) to a simple practice: using a laptop to take notes in every meeting. This approach enables me to share information promptly and accurately and provides an easy way to search through past discussions. Moreover, it ensures that I remain actively engaged in the conversation.

Unfortunately, in many meetings, active listening is a rare skill. Most attendees find themselves split between half-listening to the speaker and half-preparing their next contribution.

It's essential to note that being tardy to a meeting is not only rude but also inconsiderate. When you arrive late, you convey to the waiting participants that their time is less valuable than yours.

One of the best ways of sabotaging your own success at work is by filling your calendar up to the brim with meetings. In most companies, meetings aren't productive, so you're effectively making yourself unproductive. A self-imposed limit of 3-4 meetings a day should allow time for ad-hoc collaboration and working ON (rather than IN) the team.

My favourite joke about the importance of not being late is, "I had a brilliant time at Fight Club last night...I was a bit stressed after turning up late and missing the beginning, but Fight Club is a great white-collar boxing club on Wednesday nights in the warehouse on Main Street..."

The Team And Company Culture

A good quote is that culture eats strategy for breakfast; in reality, a company culture is just the aggregate of everyone in the company's actions and behaviours. You can't wish a culture into existence or mandate or impose it. But you can influence it by role-modelling and celebrating the positive behaviours, actions, and outcomes you value.

Culture is set by actions, not words, presentations, policies, and posters. A culture is what you do, not what you say.

Actions, not words, create cultures.

It only takes one person to poison a team culture. As Netflix founder Reed Hastings said, "Do not tolerate brilliant jerks. The cost to teamwork is too high."

I recommend the book *The 7 Habits of Highly Effective People* by Stephen Covey. It has been a classic since 1989 and is well worth a read.

If you don't have time, the habits are:

- Be Proactive
- Begin with the End in Mind
- Put First Things First
- Think Win-Win
- Seek First to Understand, Then to Be Understood
- Synergise
- Sharpen the Saw...

Early in my career, I was working at a company when our website crashed. The CTO came down to our end of the room and punched an open metal filing cabinet door. The noise reverberated across the open-plan office like a car crash, causing at least one tech team member to get up and leave. Remember, actions create culture.

One thing that characterises a team or company's culture is its attitude to risk.

Risk

Elon Musk is a risk-taker par excellence. He said, "I personally provided almost all Tesla funding, based on my proceeds from PayPal, from Series A in 2004 until Series C in 2007. In late 2008, I gave Tesla the last money I had. It was that, or the company would have died. We closed that funding round at 6pm on Christmas Eve. If we had not closed that round, Tesla would have gone bankrupt 2 days after Christmas. I gave my last money thinking Tesla would probably still die, not thinking that it would be lucrative."

Being risk-averse will slow you down, but being reckless will also often result in bad overall outcomes.

As CTO CIO, where should we aspire to be on this curve?

Maybe being risk "comfortable" is optimal in that you are comfortable with managed risks and are willing to take calculated risks in pursuit of specific goals or outcomes.

The reward for the risk is the other side of the equation, of course. The potential rewards always need to be quantified to justify the risk.

Optimise And Modernise Communication

A modern workplace collaboration tool like Slack or Workplace from Meta helps companies form a good collective identity, particularly if the teams are geographically distributed.

Slack is a great way to maintain relationships with people in teams that a CTO CIO might not normally interact with as much, such as Fulfilment and Customer Services.

Using something like Slack will reduce the number of meetings and emails you need to use to communicate and collaborate with your team, allowing you to communicate in new ways.

If you haven't already used something like Slack, introducing it will make a big difference to your company culture. It also allows people to bring their personality to work more authentically via posting in less formal channels like #random. At the time of writing, it's not expensive either; the free plan should be more than good enough to get started.

At a recent interim gig, I noticed widespread unhappiness in the Slack #customercomms channel with what I thought was an edge case in the customer sign-up process. I fixed the issue, and the customer-facing teams were over the moon. It wasn't an issue they would have ever emailed the CTO about, so I might not have heard about it without channel-based communication.

However, never underestimate the importance of remote or physical face-to-face leadership: face-to-face meetings such as having a weekly 30-minute 1:1 with direct reports, weekly ExCo meetings, quarterly all-team meetings, and annual appraisals are very important to your team members.

At Hailo, Matt Heath integrated Slackbot with the Continuous Integration/Continuous Deployment pipeline so that code could be compiled, tested, and deployed just by typing Build Somefilename in Slack.

I'm told the most effective communication I ever do is a weekly email or Slack message I like to send to my team called "Rorie's Ramblings."

It has the same format every week, including sections such as

"One Thing I Did This Week," "One Thing I Learnt This Week," "What Made Me Laugh This Week," "One Thing I Will Do Next Week," "Hat Tip Of The Week," and so on.

This email provides an excellent opportunity to enlighten your team about your weekly activities—a chance to bridge the knowledge gap, especially for junior members who might not fully grasp the responsibilities of a CTO or CIO. Beyond that, it's a platform to infuse your personality into the workplace.

Additionally, this communication presents a golden opportunity to celebrate successes (please see later for a sample).

In hard-driving cultures, it's easy to focus on problems/issues all of the time and forget to celebrate success or give praise.

At Betfair, I went as far as to put a reminder in my calendar to celebrate success every day. In a successful company, many people are doing great work, so it's normally just a question of making the time to celebrate success.

People aren't machines at the end of the day. No matter how high-performing an individual is, everyone needs recognition and encouragement to keep performing at a high level.

Offering recognition and praise carries a dual advantage. Not only does it uplift the individuals or teams receiving acknowledgment, but it also plays a pivotal role in shaping the organizational culture. Recognizing achievements is more than words; it accurately depicts the behaviors and outcomes valued, signaling a desire for more of the same.

Four-Hour Chef by Tim Ferriss is a book that is often recommended for its innovative approach to learning how to cook. It is not merely a cookbook with recipes; instead, it uses the skill of cooking to teach the reader how to learn anything efficiently.

Encourage Effective Decision Making

One of the behaviours that mark out high-performing companies and teams is the effectiveness of their decision-making. Decisions need to be:

1. Fact or data-based
   People quickly lose faith in people or organisations that can't demonstrate their decisions are logical or rational. People are happy to accept decisions they disagree with if they feel that the decision was made in the right way.
2. Made quickly...but not too quickly...
   Decisions should never be ducked or "kicked down the road." We need cultures where people and teams feel comfortable making decisions and taking accountability. It's a balance; all facts need to be considered before a decision with no "rush to judgment."
3. Made clearly and unambiguously.
   I've observed instances where individuals believe they are demonstrating cleverness by making decisions that essentially keep their options open, avoiding the need

for a definitive choice. However, this behavior can be toxic for the team and the overall culture in the long run.

4. Made collaboratively after productive debate

In one of my engagements, a religious war erupted between two opposing camps over the choice of API gateway (yes, really). To address this, I established a dedicated Slack channel where the opposing arguments were discussed constructively for about a week. Following this, we held a meeting for a comprehensive debate. As the CTO, I made the final decision on which approach we would adopt. I emphasised that the decision was now settled, and revisiting it without significant changes in our situation would be deemed unproductive.

The process left everyone relatively content, although I did make a misstep by sending out a detailed email explaining my decision so quickly after the meeting that some thought I must have written it beforehand.

One common mistake I've observed in leaders striving to appear modern and collaborative (or perhaps attempting to sidestep accountability, if I may be more cynical) is the delegation of strategic decisions to relatively junior team members.

As stated multiple times in this book, decision-making is one of the most challenging aspects of leadership. This is primarily due to the scarcity of easy decisions; in fact, the majority of decisions typically require choosing among several equally viable options. The determining factor often hinges on carefully weighing the most crucial trade-offs.

👉 Delegating strategic decisions to junior team members isn't "empowerment;" it's an abdication of leadership.

Dealing with JFDI

Under stress, some managers resort to JFDI (Just F*cking Do It) management and manage people or teams by autocratically issuing seemingly "random" orders, with no opportunity taken to give explanation or context. Sometimes the orders are inconsistent with previous JFDI orders, which is very demoralising.

Working in an environment like this can be very demotivating, and it's not easy to get managers to change their behaviour, particularly when they are under stress.

Some of the things you will need to try in this situation are as follows:

- Start logging the details of the behaviour for use in a formal process should it come to that.
- Always try to have discussions in private with JFDI managers; they are always more productive.
- Try to understand why your manager adopts this approach; it might be due to tight deadlines or pressure from above. It won't change the behaviour, but understanding what might be driving it might help deal with it.
- As a first step, constructively discuss your concerns privately with your manager and point out the impact that this management style is having on yourself, the team, productivity, and morale. Follow it up with an email recording your concerns.

- "Hi X, following up on our meeting, my team and I are finding the very directive management behaviours being exhibited at the moment very demotivating and counter-productive. We are sure that a more consultative approach would achieve better outcomes for our company, so I'm looking forward to seeing the benefits of the more structured approach we agreed upon in our meeting. Thanks."
- Politely agree on clear boundaries and a healthier WoW (Way of Working) with your manager that mitigates the downside of this approach as much as possible.
- If this approach hasn't changed the behaviours, then discuss your concerns informally with HR/the CEO/influential person. They will probably suggest some ideas which should then be tried.
- If the behaviours haven't improved, then raise a formal grievance with the CEO/HR describing the negative impacts of the behaviours.

Changing someone's behaviour is a formidable challenge. If you've exhausted all the aforementioned approaches without success, perhaps your most viable option is to consider relocating to a different team or company with a healthier work environment.

Tactics Recap

Choose 5-10 specific tactics per quarter to implement your strategies, ensuring they are actionable tasks with varying cycle times from one day to three months.

Understand the importance of cycle time as a measure of efficiency and strive to achieve low cycle times by executing well end-to-end.

Maintain a balance between achieving results and maintaining relationships, leverage a network of change agents, and avoid causing collateral damage.

The relationship between a CTO CIO and their CEO is critical. The CTO CIO should regularly include their CEO in communications and demonstrate alignment with the CEO's vision.

Focus on external customer experience and internal tool usability, actively listening to the team's ideas for improvements, and fostering a culture of effective decision-making and professionalism.

The Goal by Eliyahu M. Goldratt is a seminal book that utilises a unique narrative to introduce the theory of constraints, teaching how to identify and address bottlenecks in organisational processes.

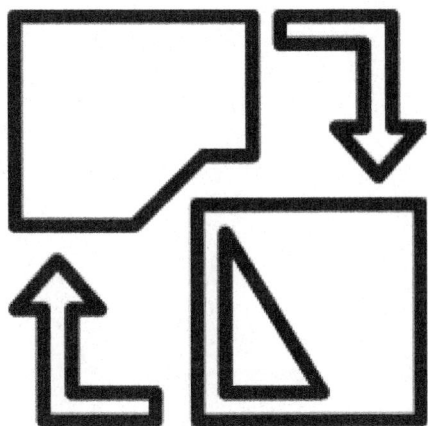

Section 9:
Game Changers

Game Changers

I've talked a lot so far about the sort of "How" tactics and strategies you might want to employ to deliver on your "What" mission and objectives. But some technologies, techniques, or approaches can have such a material impact (and are so potentially transformative) that they deserve special consideration as potential "game changers."

Let's divide them up as "People Game Changers," "Technology Game Changers," and "Process Game Changers" and look at People Game Changers first.

People Game Changers

Number One: Outsourcing

If your company has huge overcapacity or underperforming internal teams, a win/win relationship with a genuinely good outsourced provider might change the game for your company.

Of course, the outsourcing industry would have you believe that outsourcing is some sort of panacea of lower costs and better performance, but that is often far from the case.

It takes a lot of work and due diligence to create a win/win outsourcing deal. But it is possible with the right partner and contractual relationship.

Watch out for the cost of change, of course. A lot of outsourcers create an artificially positive business case by

153

charging lower upfront and ongoing costs and make their margin by overcharging for changes or quota breaches.

If you choose the right partner and get the commercial relationship right, outsourcing can be a game changer.

☛ There are a number of very public outsourcing initiative failures (such as Boeing and HSBC outsourcing their software quality assurance functions), so it goes without saying that you are dancing with the devil when you sign an outsourcing deal. The right deal can deliver real benefits, but you need to be very careful.

❗ You will probably be dealing with a huge supplier legal team experienced in creating long win/lose contracts. As I said, even if the upfront costs look attractive, be careful of the cost of change or above-quota work in your outsourcing contract.

Now, let's look at the other side of the coin;

Number Two: Insourcing

If your company has win/lose relationships with ineffective or expensive suppliers, outsourcing the work might change the game for your company. Fixing bad outsourcing relationships can increase business impact by 50% of the costs.

Watch out for the cost of extending coverage hours or enhancing SLAs when insourcing.

Good outsourcers leverage their 24-7 capabilities at a lower cost than the cost of creating or extending the hours of tech teams.

As usual, things aren't as simple as outsourcing always equals good; insourcing always equals bad (or vice versa).

What is better for you depends completely on the effectiveness of the current arrangements.

Early in your tenure, evaluate your sourcing strategy to ensure all of the internal/external relationships deliver at the right effectiveness and cost-benefit point.

Fixing an underperforming team or outsourcing relationship may be a game changer for you.

Turning Around An Underperforming Team

Turning around an underperforming team is not easy. It is probably the most common challenge I'm asked to undertake in my interim engagements.

I have successfully turned teams around on a number of occasions, so I would attack the challenge like this:

1. Interview the key stakeholders and team members 1:1 (a standard interview template is available in The Hub gro. team/cto-cio-bible-3X/hub/).

Some red flags from talking to the team and stakeholders would be the following:

- Autocratic, indecisive, ineffective, or change-averse leadership
- Bad role models in the team help perpetuate a dysfunctional culture

- A team culture that has become introspective and lost its alignment with the business's goals

- Agenda-based zealotry focusing on the sanctity of Agile principles or anything other than business impact

- An over-focus on the "How" rather than the "What" of business impact

- A low talent density with a relative lack of high performers and positive role models

- Very high average tenure with a lack of new ideas and people joining the team

A mini MOST to turn a team around might be:

Mission: Transform the team into a company asset, focusing 100% of its energy on making the company successful

Objective: Reboot the team with an unambiguous Mission, Objectives, Strategies, and Tactics.

Strategies: 1. Create target culture behaviours/actions role models 2. Manage out any negative role models 2. Augment the team with any missing critical leadership/technical skills or capabilities

Tactics: 1. Role model urgency, taking accountability, having personal effectiveness, and having a business impact focus. 2. Engineer some quick wins to demonstrate that the team is capable of good execution. 3. Make the WoW as agile as possible 4. Communicate frequently. 5. Repeat and reinforce positive behaviours until a new culture has formed.

Technology Game Changers

The Cloud

People lacking Cloud skills used to quote "Security" as an excuse not to move to The Cloud. But it is now standard practice to encrypt your data both in transit and at rest in AWS and GCP. Encryption makes your data an order of magnitude more secure than it would be in the average "old skool" physical data centre.

AWS once contacted me to tell me that one of my developers had checked in some (potentially open source) code with a query string, including the database system administrator password. The mainstream cloud providers probably have the most effective security approach and capabilities outside of the military and intelligence services.

It's very easy to waste a lot of money with cloud providers. Ensure your team carefully controls environment creation and sizing and scripts the decommissioning of environments when they're not being used overnight, on the weekend, or whenever.

API's

Creating a public application programming Interface enables businesses to take their product or service to new markets or customers and increase the value of their product or service by integrating third-party data or functionality.

The write-once/use-many-times nature of an API allows companies to leverage their IT investment by 10s or even hundreds of times.

Success was not guaranteed during the early years at Betfair. I'm convinced that creating a public API was one of the main reasons it beat the imitators and competition. (It eventually went public on the London Stock Exchange for £1.5 Billion). Moneyfarm recently announced the largest API-based digital wealth management partnership in Europe.

Cross-Platform App Approaches

I have successfully used cross-platform approaches like PWA and React Native to deliver native app-like experiences from a largely consolidated code base. (In other words, there are no completely separate web, iOS Swift, or Android Kotlin code bases). This obviously can save considerable amounts of time or money, and the customer experience is very similar for most use cases. The React Native code calls the same operating system hooks as native code, providing a very "native-like" experience.

PWAs

Creating a single Progressive Web App will allow you to deliver web and native iOS and Android app-like experiences from one integrated web and app tech platform. That could deliver a 66% cost saving or a 300% increase in development velocity.

Apple's Safari implementation of PWA isn't as good as Google's Chrome implementation. But there aren't any issues that can't be fixed with a bit of JavaScript. AlaaS. Team is a PWA.

Turning a web page into a PWA isn't as hard as you might think. All you need to do is create a JSON manifest file (showing where the static assets are), the service-worker JavaScript, and put a couple of tags in the HTML pointing to them.

I wouldn't write a mobile game using cross-platform technology. But for most use cases, it's possible to use a cross-platform technology to create engaging user experiences for a fraction of the time and money needed to create and maintain three separate (Web/iOS/Android) code bases.

Google Go/golang

As described elsewhere, in Golang, Google has created a back-end platform services language that is easier to learn, code, and deploy faster and more cost-effective than all of the alternatives.

At Hailo, we re-platformed from PHP & Java to a golang micro-services platform. We saw a 60% reduction in AWS cost per transaction as we scaled up past 1,000,000 users...

AI

Writing in late 2023, it's hard to remember such a disruptive change as the rise of AI LLMs (Large Language Models) since the release of ChatGPT in November 2022. Like the personal computer or smartphone, "AI" has changed the game forever.

I'm no dilettante when it comes to AI; my undergraduate dissertation was on "Using Neural Networks for financial time series prediction." Yes, they had neural networks way back when I was an undergraduate (ahem).

I have experienced notable success in predicting time series data, such as unemployment rates, but encountered challenges when dealing with noisy datasets like intraday GBP to $ exchange rates. Similar to the evolution of technologies like the cloud and big data, AI has traversed a hype cycle, and it appears that we are now witnessing its realisation.

Services like OpenAI's ChatGPT demonstrate the efficacy of a neural network approach when extensively trained on vast datasets. For instance, GPT-4 reportedly utilises a dataset of 1 petabyte and boasts 300 billion parameters.

In my attempt to demystify neural networks and their functioning, I've provided an explanation on The Hub at gro. team/cto-cio-bible-3X/hub/.

As a CTO/CIO, the question arises: How can AI be leveraged to create a competitive advantage for your company, and can it truly deliver business impact now? The answer is affirmative. In one of my engagements, neural network predictive models successfully predicted customer behaviors such as churn propensity, additional product purchases, and increased investment, yielding positive ROI.

While Language Model Models (LLMs) like ChatGPT are not a form of superintelligence threatening redundancy, they possess the potential to significantly enhance productivity. Every business leader should be actively experimenting and learning with AI.

In recent AIaaS.Team engagements, LLMs have been employed to automatically generate up-sell/cross-sell emails based on unstructured data, expedite the creation of legal documents compared to existing expert systems, and analyze physical and financial assets, among other applications.

WordPress Elementor

Despite the prevalent snobbery towards WordPress within the IT community, leveraging Elementor to build a straightforward website offers a significant advantage in terms of speed, quality, and cost-effectiveness compared to traditional methods. This holds true, of course, with the exception of the emerging AI-powered tools. The extensive WordPress plugin ecosystem further facilitates the creation of sophisticated functionality or capabilities within WordPress, often quickly and straightforwardly.

Do not use WordPress custom themes. They were invented by web design agencies to lock clients in and deliver a recurring revenue stream by making clients dependent on them for any and all upgrades and changes. Choose a standard theme; there are thousands to choose from.

The WordPress plug-in ecosystem is Achille's heel as well. The plug-ins are created by developers from all over the world with unverifiable security capabilities and rigour. Don't store any data in a WordPress database that would cause reputational harm if it were leaked, and make sure all plug-ins are always set to auto-update to the latest version.

📖 *Zero to One* by Peter Thiel offers unique insights into the mindset and strategy needed to create innovative and monopolistic businesses that will shape the future. It's required reading for entrepreneurs and innovators looking to build the next great company.

No Code

At the time of writing, no code platforms such as bubble.io might just be about to go mainstream and be quicker, better, and cheaper for some use cases in which we're essentially just mashing up different external capabilities. Emerging platforms like durable.co make it super easy to create websites, so it's an area worth keeping a close eye on.

Caching

Caching is unglamorous, but an effective caching strategy can have a transformative effect in an IT ecosystem. Edge, disk, database, and memory caching can all decrease latency, increase capacity, and save money.

Process Game Changers

👉 Leveraging a modern SaaS CRM platform (such as HubSpot or Salesforce) can change the game for some businesses. The capabilities they make available at reasonable (HubSpot) and unreasonable (Salesforce) costs are way ahead of what anything but the biggest businesses could have enjoyed even a few years ago.

Avoid customising the code of ERP and CRM platforms like the plague. You will probably lose your ability to take advantage of core product developments without more customisation.

One of my clients extensively customised their SAP system during its implementation, leading to a situation where upgrading became financially prohibitive. Consequently, they found themselves locked into the same version of SAP, facing this challenge for over 12 years – a situation no organization desires.

While custom data fields/objects are essential and often necessary, the key principle is to configure rather than code. Including a developer in your ERP implementation team could be a significant mistake, as it deviates from the best practice of emphasizing configuration over coding.

You are dancing with the devil when you implement an ERP system. If you standardise your business processes to match the software (rather than the other way around) and avoid custom point-to-point interfaces to other systems, then maybe, just maybe, the ERP system may not ultimately be an expensive and inflexible constraint on your business.

Ned Hasovic (CTO & Co-Founder at Cambrian Games) says, "To a CTO, everything matters, especially product. Sanity check whether Epics and the Micro are meaningful to the customer and the business before the technology macro is laid out".

! ERP systems are the fast food of the IT world; they look so simple, quick, and enticing but normally end up making their consumers less agile, poorer, and unable to compete.

Game Changers Recap

Outsourcing as a People Game Changer: It can be transformative if managed properly with the right partner and contractual terms. However, there is a risk of hidden costs, particularly with changes and quota breaches. Notable failures like Boeing and HSBC's software quality assurance functions caution the need for careful consideration.

Insourcing as a Reversal Strategy: Reverting back from ineffective or expensive outsourcing can lead to significant cost savings and increased business impact but requires careful management of coverage hours and service level agreements (SLAs).

Turning Around an Underperforming Team: This common challenge involves understanding the team and stakeholder dynamics, identifying issues such as weak leadership or a misaligned culture, and implementing strategic changes to align the team's mission with the company's goals for a turnaround.

Technology Game Changers: Adoption of cloud services, APIs, cross-platform apps, PWAs (Progressive Web Apps), the Go language, and AI, particularly AI LLMs (Large Language Models) like ChatGPT, can significantly enhance security, reduce costs, and increase

---

development velocity, offering the potential to drastically transform business operations.

Process Innovations and Warnings: Utilizing modern SaaS platforms can be a game changer, but customization of ERP and CRM systems should be avoided. Implementing ERP systems should be done cautiously to avoid creating inflexibility and decreasing the company's ability to compete.

No-code platforms are on the rise as a potential mainstream solution for integrating various external capabilities.

As Artur Grabowski (a Technical Leader, Engineer, and Technology Allrounder CTO) says, "If there's any advice I could give to people starting their careers as CTOs, it would be that their role is more about building bridges than anything else. It's not just about technology; technology is the least of the problems, and solutions can be found for any technical challenge. Communication is key. Regardless of how the company is set up, difficulties in delivery and product understanding will arise, both on the technology and product sides. Building bridges and filling knowledge gaps will be crucial. Make no mistake, there will be people who prefer using shoelaces instead of metal or concrete to build bridges, and sometimes, there's little you can do about it. In such cases, the only thing you can ensure is to replace the shoelace with something better the next time it fails."

Section 10: The CTO CIO Career & Personal Brand

Building A CTO CIO Career And Personal Brand

Getting Promoted To A CTO CIO Role

Getting promoted to CTO CIO is not easy; it's one of those roles (like CMO Chief Marketing Officer) that can make or break a business, so the expectations of people in this role can be very high.

I wish I had a pound every time I have heard, "If only our technology and/or marketing team was better, then we'd be successful with our hockey stick growth plan."

CTO and CIO are also roles that mean different things to different people (covered later), so it's easy to end up in a situation where the CTO CIO isn't meeting stakeholder expectations.

So, how do you get promoted to CTO CIO?

Realistically, I think you have a better chance of being promoted to CTO CIO within your company than being appointed as a first-time CTO CIO at a new company.

That's not 100% the case, though. Sometimes, if you have a particularly strong domain or relevant technology knowledge, a company will take a chance on you and hire you as CTO CIO. Working at a respected competitor can be a good way to get promoted like this.

So, what should you do to get promoted?

I think the most important thing you can do to get promoted to CTO CIO is to act like a good CTO CIO *now*.

The titles of CTO or CIO are not prerequisites for being an exceptional technology leader. In your current role, guide your team on a mission to drive business impact. Empower and develop your team members, infuse energy, optimism, and passion into the work environment, simplify processes to bring clarity, and foster clear, frequent collaboration and communication.

As long as you make sure that the business impact you want to lead is aligned with your CTO CIO's mission, then by leading change in your current role, you will be making a great step toward being a CTO CIO one day.

The changes you lead will also give you great case studies and credentials during a CTO CIO interview process.

A CTO CIO is also a role model for their team, so at a personal level, you should strive to have a high degree of personal effectiveness. Be reliable and trustworthy: say what you do, and do what you say.

As I've said before, one of the things that I feel really contributes to my effectiveness is taking notes on my laptop during meetings. It forces me to listen and creates an accurate record of decisions/facts that I can search and share quickly and easily.

So, in summary, to get promoted to CTO CIO, start acting like one *now*. If you do that, it will only be a matter of time before you are promoted or have a credible track record when interviewing with a new company.

At one of my engagements, the CMO used to call the CMO and CTO roles "danger money" and say that once appointed, the clock is ticking until you get fired in these roles in particular. It is a bit like being a football manager/coach. If the results aren't as the "owners" expected, it will be Marketing and/or Tech's fault.

What Is The Difference Between A CTO and CIO?

There is no right, wrong, or universally accepted definition of what a CTO (Chief Technology Officer) is, what a CIO (Chief Information Officer) is, or what the difference between the two roles is.

Some companies have a CTO, some companies have a CIO, and some even have a number of people with one or more of these job titles across their (usually large) organisation. It is generally agreed that both of these job titles entail running a "Technology"/"IT" Team as the most senior IT person in the business.

I recommend the book *The Hard Thing About Hard Things* by Ben Horowitz as an excellent reflection on Ben's experiences across a number of startups. The standout quote is, "If you're going to eat sh*t, don't nibble"...

Of course, a company wants and needs both the "CTO" ¦ "CIO" perspectives to varying degrees during different stages of its growth. It's why having a CIO and CTO might be an optimum structure once a company has reached a big scale or complexity.

What is a CTO

A Chief Technology Officer could be said to have a bias to working "IN" the team rather than "ON" the team.

They might be biased to look "IN" rather than "OUT" from the tech team. They should be passionate about existing and emerging technologies and how they can be used to create a competitive advantage for their company. They might read Hacker News and Slashdot and have and use a GitHub account.

A good CTO will have kept their core technical skills up to date. They won't have the time or experience to do every person's job in their team, but they will have maintained a core set of technical skills that are up-to-date and relevant.

They might have come up through the more "technical" routes of architect, development manager, developer, etc. They are also normally the company's lead technology evangelist and advocate.

As Richard Max (Technical Leadership: AI, Blockchain, Marketing, Publishing & Product (Web4+3+2)) says:

"The most important tech things I've learnt as I grow older have come from the youngest and most inexperienced members of a team. Ignore them at your peril!"

What is a CIO?

❗ A Chief Information Officer could be said to have a bias to working "ON" the team rather than "IN" the team.

They might have a bias to look "OUT" rather than "IN" from the IT/Tech Team. They should focus on getting a positive return on investment from the company's technology spending. A CIO might dispassionately view the IT Team as just one of the teams in the company that needs to be cost-effective and deliver the company's business plan. They might read forbes.com, wsj.com and are thinking about doing an MBA one day.

They might have come up through the less "technical" routes of Service Delivery, Programme Director, Project Manager, etc. They view technology as a "HOW," not a "WHAT".

📖 I recommend the book co-written by the captain of a US nuclear submarine *Turn The Ship Around!: A True Story of Building Leaders* by Breaking the Rules by L. David Marquet and Stephen R Covey. It is an excellent description of how empowering people can fundamentally change team performance.

I've done a number of jobs as both CTO and CIO, trying to work the same way with both job titles. Everything worked out OK for me, so maybe we shouldn't get too hung up on any perceived difference in the job titles...

Suggested 100-day Plan

Congratulations on your new leadership role!

Creating a 100-day plan is an excellent way to hit the ground running and make a positive impact quickly.

Let's create a mini MOST to help you structure what you might want to accomplish in your first hundred days.

Our **Mission** is to hit the ground running and make a positive impact during my first 100 days

Objectives:

- Get to know my team
- Understand my business
- Create and communicate my team's MOST
- Start to build relationships
- Deliver some quick wins to start to build my reputation

Strategies:

- Spend time with my direct reports and key team members to understand their roles, responsibilities, strengths, and weaknesses. Schedule regular one-on-one meetings with each direct report and ExCo member to build rapport, listen to their feedback, and better understand the company's history and culture. Schedule regular team check-ins and monthly team town halls to keep everyone informed and engaged.
- Dive deep into the company's financials, products, services, and customers. Review any reports, plans, or strategies developed by my predecessor. Analyse the

competitive landscape and identify areas for growth and improvement.

- Communicate my mission, objectives, and strategies clearly and consistently with my team, peers, and stakeholders. Make sure that people understand my goals and priorities.
- Develop relationships with key stakeholders, such as customers, partners, investors, ExCo, and board members. Meet with them regularly to understand their perspectives and expectations.
- Look for low-hanging fruit and quick wins that can boost morale, productivity, or revenue quickly. Implement them as soon as possible to build momentum and demonstrate leadership.

Tactics

The tactics will really depend on your context. But a great place to start is to look to implement at least some of the suggestions interviewees might have offered in response to questions like "What is the first thing you would do if you were the new CTO CIO?"

Don't underestimate the positive impact of removing or changing a long-running problem or irritation, however minor it appears, coming in cold. It shows you listen and follow through on what you say.

At one of my engagements, all the employees hated the locked-down, old-fashioned corporate Wintel standard-built laptop that "IT" mandated that they use. I added an option for employees to use an Apple MacBook because when you ran the numbers and added up the cost of the Intel machine, docking station, and Windows software a MacBook + support was cheaper. Yes, cheaper. After we did that, they practically erected a statue to "IT" in the car park.

A really useful thing to do in your first 100 days is to talk directly to your company's customers. Listen to phone calls, accompany salespeople during customer visits, or do whatever makes sense in your company. As you implement your changes, check in with customers regularly to measure the impact your changes are having.

I learnt a lot during a couple of days accompanying the salespeople as they visited local businesses to encourage them to renew their annual Yell (Yellow Pages) advertising package. Every customer said, "I don't want to renew advertising in the book," and every single one of them did. I came away from the day with a huge amount of respect for the salespeople and lots of ideas on how we could improve their clunky laptop-based ERP front-end system with modern tablet web-based tools.

Don't forget to measure, act, measure: Continuously evaluate your progress against your MOST and adjust your plan accordingly. Be agile, flexible, and adaptable as circumstances change.

Remember, your 100-day plan is just the beginning of your leadership journey. Use it as a foundation to build lasting relationships, make meaningful contributions, and achieve long-term success in your new role.

Oras Al-Kubaisi (CTO at Figg Wealth) says, "Visualise the finish line but focus on the next step only. Marginal gains are underrated."

Donut Economics by Kate Raworth is interesting for its fresh approach to economic thinking, challenging traditional models and suggesting a sustainable framework that balances human needs with planetary boundaries.

Success as an Interim/Freelancer/Consultant

If you're considering moving into a more "flexible" variable capacity employment arrangement, what should you do to maximise your chances of success?

In my experience, very few people are treated differently in interim roles than "permanent" employees. The fact that you're an interim won't be a big issue, but their expectations of you as an interim can sometimes be higher.

You might be expected to be an expert on more things, and you'll probably be expected to have a measurable impact – perhaps more quickly than a new full-time employee would be.

You could also get more latitude to challenge the orthodoxy, not be expected to navigate the company politics so carefully and have your change agenda considered more dispassionately.

So, how do you ensure success in your first interim consultant role? The first (and maybe obvious) point is to choose the right role.

During your first week, make an effort to meet as many team members as possible. Building rapport is crucial; scheduling 30-minute interviews with each team member can provide valuable insights. Asking thoughtful questions during these sessions will help you quickly understand the dynamics and challenges of the team, facilitating a smoother integration.

There is a suggested template at gro.team/cto-cio-bible-3X/hub/, but the suggested interview questions are:

- Are you enjoying it here at the moment?
- What are our key responsibilities as a team?
- As a team, what do you think we do well?
- What do we need to get better at?
- Who are our stars?
- Does anyone need help to be more successful?
- How could we get even more customer outcome-focused?
- How could we move faster?
- Would you recommend working here to a friend?
- What three things would you do if you were me?
- Is there anything else we should talk about?

Making sure you understand whether you will need to be a good cultural fit or be counter-cultural is one of the reasons why they want to hire you. When you start, get the basics right. Always arrive on time and dress similarly to the prevailing dress code in the team.

❗ At the early stages of any assignment, ensure you don't write cheques you can't cash by promising unachievable things. There is no surer way of destroying your credibility (and making enemies of other people) than by promising things that can't be delivered. It's a subtle situation, though. You may have been brought in to increase urgency and delivery, so any goals you agree on need to be ambitious but achievable.

When you arrive, the most important thing to do is to listen. Never make the mistake of joining with a "here's the solution: now tell me about the problem" approach.

👉 Don't set yourself up for failure by taking an interim role with a team size, company culture, or business model you're not absolutely confident you can add real value to. Ultimately, what you "sell" is your reputation and track record – don't be tempted to risk it by taking on a role you're not 100% right for.

Once you have found the right role, and before you start, ensure you are very clear about the brief. Ensure you understand what success will look like in the potential role. Sometimes companies want a change agent, but sometimes they just want someone to "act like they got the job for real" and do their "sensible best."

After the interviews, an interesting exercise is to allocate any team member mentioned as a "star" in Question 5 with a plus 1 and any struggling team member mentioned in Question 6 with a minus 1. Adding up all the scores will give a quick but surprisingly accurate team talent map. Question 9 can also be used to create a quick team "Net Promoter Score."

At GRO.TEAM, we like to end the first week of a new assignment with a "Week One Playback" with the person who sponsored the appointment. It's a great opportunity to discuss the SWOT (Strengths, Weaknesses, Opportunities, Threats) found so far and calibrate it against what the sponsor wants.

Also, remember to add value to your client in any way you can. It's not just about the day-to-day goals. Doing things like sharing their job postings on LinkedIn, mentioning them in any interviews you do, retweeting their tweets, liking their Facebook page, and so on all help.

Don't "penny-pinch" the client, either. What "goes around comes around," so if taking a phone call or sending a quick email in non-client chargeable time helps solve a problem or keep momentum up, then do it. You'll be judged on your impact at the end of the day.

The last thing to remember is to know when to move on. You know when you've achieved your goals or hit the diminishing returns point on the value curve. Don't wait to be replaced. Proactively suggest a new way to add value for the client if one is appropriate, or move on to your next challenge with another successful engagement under your belt.

So there you have it. To be a successful interim or freelance consultant, you need to choose the right role, deliver as much value as possible, and move on as soon as you've done it.

We summarise it at GRO.TEAM with our motto of "Be Of Value."

If you do that at all times, you will be successful.

Saranjit Soor (CTO at Equivo) says, "Have the difficult conversations as early as possible. It leaves more time to work on solutions. Also obsess about value, value to the business, value to the team, how much of an impact will changes make and how quickly".

Running And Changing A CTO CIO Career And Personal Brand

People make a career by telling people how to develop their personal brand, and I'm no specialist. But to me, the really important issues are:

- Think about what you want your authentic brand to be. Do you want to be an SME (subject matter expert) in a particular field, or be considered a thought leader on general leadership, or whatever?
- Post on LinkedIn and or Twitter as often as you can find the time, at least once a week. You need to put the work in to build up your online presence; it takes considerable effort.

To quote the 80s TV programme Fame, "Fame costs... and right here is where you start paying..."

- I don't see the ROI of TikTok, Instagram, Facebook, and the other platforms in a professional context, but I guess that will be different if your business's target markets are using these platforms

- Try to post interesting or useful content; do as little "humble bragging" as possible
- Make sure you are consistent in your online "voice" and really are authentic. It is obvious when people are being "corporate" or insincere
- It's easy to focus on "vanity metrics" like the number of followers on social media, but that isn't the goal. It might make you feel good, but having thousands of fake followers who never really hire you or buy your product/service doesn't help you. Focus on quality, not quantity.

Linked in With over a billion users, LinkedIn is now unquestionably the primary professional social media platform to manage your career and personal brand.

I'm no social media specialist, but LinkedIn invited me to participate in their Editorial Programme for Creators. Hopefully, I have some "insider" knowledge I can share.

Using LinkedIn Effectively

- Post frequently; building a network and brand takes tenacity

- Adding video to your posts increases engagement
- Use AI to create images (ChatGPT 4.5) or videos (latte. social) for your posts
- Encourage comments by tagging people likely to engage and asking questions at the end of posts. Apparently, the LinkedIn algorithm values comments over likes and shares.

- Be a good LinkedIn citizen by commenting on and sharing other people's posts. I'm told the LinkedIn algorithm penalises people whose posts to comments/likes ratio is too high. But I don't know how true that is.
- Adding 3-5 hashtags to your posts is optimum, apparently, but I normally forget to do that.

> Sorry, there are no shortcuts. Post consistently and often; building a network and brand takes persistence.

X, still known as Twitter, is the best (and funniest) platform to follow what is happening in your industry, field, or area.

- Create separate "professional" and anonymous "burner" accounts on which you can follow politicians, personal causes, and so on. I think staying neutral in the online culture war (and away from any and all divisive issues) is the optimum approach for your career.
- I tend to be "read-only" on Twitter but have had a few half-hearted attempts at building a Twitter following over the years. I have just launched a new personal account (@RorieDevine if you want to follow me) because "people like people," and personal accounts seem to do better. Let's see how it goes; I might have already given up again by the time you read this (ahem).
- Don't forget that what you post and who you follow on Twitter is essentially public and lasts forever. There have been many cases in which people have lost or failed to land jobs because of things they posted on Twitter years ago.

☛ I know it's obvious, but don't post anything once you have started drinking alcohol. Many people have "come a cropper" doing that. James May of Top Gear fame has a "corks out, phones down" rule.

- Follow the thought leaders actively posting in your industry or area. The quality and timeliness of the insight available for free is very, very high
- Building a Twitter following can be challenging, and many successful individuals often recount a journey where they consistently posted for 18-24 months with minimal engagement, akin to a 'tumbleweed' effect. Eventually, they reach a tipping point, and engagement suddenly takes off, growing exponentially. It's worth noting that many individuals may give up before reaching that tipping point.
- There are services out there that promise to grow your Twitter follower count, but I wouldn't bother with them. They all seem to work by following lots of people known to be likely to "follow back." It might work in the short term to get your follower count up. But you would only have a very low-quality network of people not genuinely interested in you or your content.

How Should You Spend Your Time?

This is the sort of approach you might want to take:

Monday **AM** Direct Reports meeting **PM** 1:1 ExCo 1:1 CEO

Tuesday **AM** Direct Reports 1:1s, Celebrate Success

Wednesday **AM** Celebrate success, Direct Reports 1:1s

Thursday **AM** Direct Reports 1:1s **PM** ExCo 1:1s, celebrate Success

Friday **PM** Send/Post "Ramblings" Email/Slack

Take every opportunity to celebrate success during the week.

At one engagement, I became famous amongst my ExCo colleagues for always starting 1:1s with the question, "Is anything vexing you?" I find this question always gets to the important issues without "beating around the bush."

Don't overstuff your diary with meetings. Try to keep at least 2-3 hours a day meeting free to do some actual work. Many people fail because they equate meetings with work and, therefore, think the more meetings they have, the more productive they are. In actual fact, the opposite is true: meetings are a "How," not a "What," and you need to focus on the "What."

Sample Rorie's Ramblings Missive

One Thing I Did This Week @here

I started at client X this week. They are a great bunch with a lot to do if they want to be the digital business they aspire to be. Overall, it's very similar to the situation at other client Y. There is plenty of opportunity for us to have an impact. Watch this space.

Stat Of The Week

£100k is what one vendor charged the client for basically a WordPress-responsive website form wrapped as an app to allow people to lodge insurance claims on their phones.

Another Thing I Did This Week

I agreed to run a Digital Boardroom on becoming an Interim for CIO Watercooler this week on Monday lunchtime. Please feel free to join in! You will need to have registered on https://ciowatercooler.co.uk/

Hat Tip Of The Week

Hats off to @sue this week for taking on the challenge of creating Android and iOS hybrid apps from responsive websites and nailing it! It just shows what you can do if you put your mind to it, and hopefully, now Sales will sell bucketloads of them.

What Made Me Laugh This Week

I found myself at the airport at an ungodly hour on Monday, en route to Copenhagen, when I unexpectedly crossed paths with the CEO (because who doesn't want to run into their boss at 5:30 am?). Seizing the opportunity, we decided to grab a coffee, and I thought it was the perfect chance to showcase my fintech prowess with my brand-new, sleek, and seriously cool Revolut metal card.

However, as it turned out, it was the first time I had used the card, and it needed to be inserted into the machine. That's when things took an unexpected turn. Despite its swanky appearance, the card turned out to be too thick for some POS terminals and even cash point machines, as I later discovered. So there I was, looking far from cool, struggling to insert my supposedly impressive card into a machine. Lesson learned – perhaps trying to show off wasn't the best idea after all.

Career Self Check List

Creating a career self-checklist is a great way to double-check that you're doing the right thing and the thing right.

Here are the things you might want to look at:

Doing The Right Thing

- Identify your strengths and weaknesses
- Evaluate your interests, values, and passions
- Consider skills that you enjoy using and those you want to develop
- Are you doing something that 1. You really enjoy 2. That you're really good at, and 3. Can you finance the lifestyle you want doing?

Career Goals

- Define medium-term (1-2 years) and long-term (5-10 years) career goals
- Be specific about what you want to achieve (e.g., a certain position, skillset, or industry)

Skill Development

- Identify key skills required for your desired career path
- Plan how to acquire or enhance these skills (e.g., courses, workshops, self-study)

Networking

- Make a list of networking activities (attending industry events, joining professional groups)

- Identify individuals in your network who could provide guidance or mentorship

CV/Resume and Online Presence

- Regularly update your resume to reflect new skills and experiences
- Ensure your LinkedIn and other professional profiles are up-to-date

Job Market Research

- Stay informed about trends and demands in your industry
- Research companies and roles that align with your career goals

Work-Life Balance

- Assess your current work-life balance
- Set goals for maintaining or improving this balance

Personal Development

- Include personal growth goals (e.g., improving communication skills and leadership abilities)
- Consider activities outside of work that contribute to personal development (e.g., volunteering, hobbies)

Feedback and Reflection

- Seek feedback from colleagues, mentors, or bosses
- Regularly reflect on your career progress and adjust your goals as needed

Financial Planning

- Evaluate your current financial situation in relation to your career
- Set financial goals that support your career objectives (e.g., saving for further education, investing in a home office)

Building, Running, and Changing a CTO CIO Career And Personal Brand Recap

CTO/CIO Promotion:

The most favorable opportunities for promotion to CTO or CIO often arise internally. However, possessing strong domain knowledge or experience with a respected competitor can open doors externally. Demonstrating leadership qualities and aligning with the current CTO or CIO's mission can significantly enhance your chances of promotion.

Differences Between CTO and CIO:

The distinction between CTO and CIO roles varies between companies, and the titles are frequently used interchangeably. Generally, a CTO maintains a technical focus and core technical skills, while a CIO leans more towards a business-oriented perspective, emphasising ROI from technology investments. Literature on both roles underscores the importance of empowerment and effective people management.

100-Day Plan:

For those stepping into new leadership roles, a recommended plan involves familiarising oneself with the team, comprehending the business landscape, setting and communicating objectives, building relationships, and achieving quick wins to establish a positive reputation.

Interim/Freelance Success:

Achieving success in interim or freelance roles necessitates selecting the right position, understanding the cultural dynamics, delivering measurable impact, and upholding credibility through realistic and achievable goal-setting.

Managing Career and Personal Brand:

Authenticity is paramount in personal branding, with regular engagement on professional platforms like LinkedIn being highly advisable. Prioritising the quality of connections over quantity is crucial. Clear career goals, continuous skill development, and maintaining a healthy work-life balance are also suggested practices.

📖 *Life 3.0* by Max Tegmark is worth a read for its thought-provoking exploration of the future of artificial intelligence and its potential impact on the very fabric of human existence, society, and ethics.

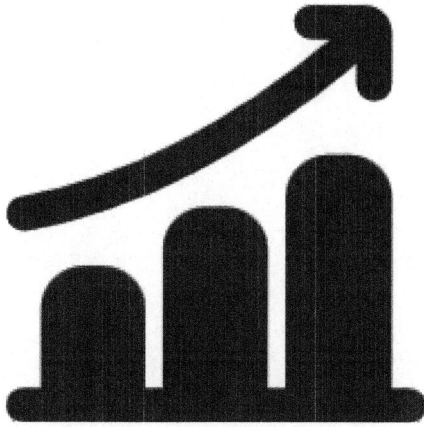

Section 11:
Growth Hacking

Growth Hacking

I've included a section about growth hacking in *The CTO | CIO Bible 3X* to show how easily the techniques and approaches used in Agile software development can be applied in other areas. Please feel free to skip this section if that isn't of interest to you right now.

☛ The same underlying principles that make Agile software development so effective also mean Growth Hacking can totally transform the effectiveness of a company's growth initiatives.

All good CTO CIOs are directly or indirectly involved in generating business growth, and the good news is that you already have a great tool in your toolbox that you can use.

Agile development massively increased the value delivered by the typical software development project by favouring "individuals and interactions" over specification, "working software" over pretty much everything, "customer collaboration" over contract negotiations, and "responding to change" over blindly following a plan.

What would happen if we used these "Agile" principles to deliver growth rather than Software?!? We could favour "customer collaboration" and "individuals and interactions" by forming a cross-functional growth team including both "customers" and "suppliers." We should include representatives from Product, Sales, Marketing, Technology, Operations, Finance, etc.

In our case, we could favour "working software" or growth by giving the team the single unifying purpose of growing a carefully chosen growth metric. The Growth Team could be "responding to change" rather than following a plan by delivering early and taking a measure-act-measure approach to ideas through on-ramp to live stages.

The Growth Team could communicate and meet regularly; maybe a quick "stand up" at the same time and place every day would work well. We could work to a weekly or fortnightly rhythm with the cumulative effects of the growth activities on the Growth metric being publicly demonstrated (and hopefully celebrated) at the end of every cycle or "sprint."

So, we have created a cross-functional team meeting regularly with the unified common purpose of doing anything and everything necessary to measure their ideas' impact on a single carefully chosen growth metric. That's cool, but maybe we could give this sort of approach a name:

Like Growth Hacking or something?

Growth Hacking is the sort of term that means different things to different people. However, anyone familiar with Agile software development will be struck by the similarities between the approaches, rituals, and rhythms typically used in Growth Hacking and Agile software development. Does it all work in the real world? Yes.

☞ Whether you call it Growth Hacking or something else, a very effective way of accelerating your growth is to learn from agile software development and to create a cross-functional team meeting regularly with the unified common purpose of doing anything and everything necessary to measure the impact of their ideas on a single carefully chosen growth metric.

Section 12: The Biggest Mistakes Of My Career

The Biggest Mistakes Of My Career...
And what I learnt from them...

The Mistake

Early in my career, I was working as a consultant implementing derivatives trading floor systems, living and working in Frankfurt, Germany. I was working in a side room just off the trading floor of a famous German bank, and thinking I was working on a test system issued a Unix "kill -9" command to kill the processes and take the system down. I realised something was wrong when I heard shrieks from the trading floor, followed by the bank's manager running in to ask what had happened. I had accidentally killed the live system. I brought it back online as quickly as possible whilst offering profuse apologies.

What I Learnt

Be very careful when working simultaneously on live and test systems. I habitually configured live windows/tabs with a red background to remind myself I was working on the live system. Thankfully, I never did it again in my career. Create safety-net cues to help avoid mistakes.

The Mistake

I was working for a client building a data-driven banking system but was sometimes experiencing irretrievable customer data loss during customer onboarding. Data loss is always a bad thing, but it is particularly bad in a banking system.

What I Learnt

The system had been built with a synchronous processing flow utilising serverless components. The serverless cold start time of up to one second was eventually identified as the root cause. In this engagement, I learnt that systems should be asynchronous (ideally idempotent) and that serverless is a great approach and technology for prototypes and POCs but probably should be avoided on live systems. Particularly OLTP systems.

The Mistake

Betfair, now part of Flutter, operated as a person-to-person betting exchange where individuals could place bets on the occurrence ('Back') or non-occurrence ('Lay') of events. A significant issue arose when a software release led to Back bets being incorrectly categorized as Lay bets, essentially the opposite of what the customer intended. This scenario, where customer expectations were reversed, was arguably one of the most undesirable outcomes.

What I Learnt

The new software had only been released to one market—a mid-week mid-afternoon greyhound market, so literally only one bet of £35 was affected. We rolled back the release and credited the bet as if it had won. By laser targeting releases, we could avoid being risk averse and still "move fast and break things," confident in the knowledge that breaking something wouldn't cause massive financial or reputational damage.

The Mistake

Possibly the most embarrassing situation I have been involved in was a project to create new payment rails for a new product. The payment rail had been used in the past, so it was assumed it was fine, and genuine E2E testing wasn't performed. As it turned out, the payment rail had been repurposed post-Brexit, so there was a nasty surprise a few weeks before launch when it was discovered that a fundamental part of the product's capability was missing.

What I Learnt

Always do genuine end-to-end testing; the earlier, the better. Put it at the beginning of the project plan and the end.

The Mistake

About 18 months after graduating, I was working for a well-known consultancy company, managing a small team of two onsite at a large client. One day, the Head of IT from the client's side approached me, requesting a membership list containing current and past member names and addresses. Without giving it much thought, I promptly wrote an SQL query and generated the file for him. It wasn't until about three months later that the repercussions became evident. The head office was inundated with complaints from people who had received loyalty cards for their deceased partners. The ensuing scandal was significant, leading to a surge in phone calls, a furious client, and the situation teetering on the brink of making it into the newspapers.

What I Learnt

When writing the SQL, I forgot to check whether the member was deceased. That day, I learnt two things: 1. Always understand why you're doing something, and make sure the "release" process matches the risk/reward of the task, and 2. The importance of relationships. The company's Head of IT could have "thrown me under the bus," but he protected me because he liked me and the other work I had been doing.

Section 13: The Characteristics Of A Successful Leader

The Characteristics Of A Successful Leader

I've worked with a lot of successful leaders in my career and a fair number of unsuccessful ones, so here is my very subjective list of the typical characteristics of a successful leader:

- They are physically fit, making time for exercise in their schedules no matter how busy they are. I think I'm right in saying that exercise and meditation are the only two ways to rewire the neurons in your brain. I have certainly had some of my best ideas whilst trundling on a treadmill. Exercise also helps you cope with stress, and of course, it's much better for you than any other self-medication, like unhealthy food, alcohol, or drugs.
- They are optimistic and energetic, bringing energy and optimism to work every day. Everyone has good and bad days, but great leaders park their troubles much better than others and are always a positive energy "source," not "sink."
- They have a sense of humour. Laughter is a great ice-breaker; people like working with people who laugh and make them laugh.
- They have low ego. The "old skool" arrogant "ego" CEO should be long gone by now. To succeed in these more "networked" times, you must create, leverage, and value

relationships with other people. That is hard if you think you are better than everyone else in some way.

- They bring their personality to work. We spend a lot of time working (particularly in high-growth or high-challenge situations), and we all want to work with people who bring all aspects of their personality to work. Distance and/or formality no longer work as well in the modern workplace.

Summary

With any luck, you have picked up some tools, techniques, or ideas to become a successful CTO CIO or be even more successful if you are already in the role. In this book, we talked about the need for you to role model a focus on business impact, to conceive and lead change, how structuring your change agenda within a M.O.S.T. framework will almost certainly help, how you should strive to create competitive advantage for your company, and how to be successful you should bring optimism, urgency, clarity and delivery and increase agility, simplicity, and accountability.

To me, an effective leader:

- Role models the actions and behaviours that they value
- Co-creates a genuinely impactful Mission
- Leads their team on that Mission to move the needle for their business
- Challenges and engages their team members

- Brings energy, optimism, humour, and passion to the team
- Simplifies everything, always increasing focus and clarity
- Collaborates and communicates authentically, clearly and often

You won't go far wrong if you do some or most of these things.

Sample M.O.S.T. templates are available in The Hub gro.team/cto-cio-bible-3X/hub/, so have a look at them and have a go creating a M.O.S.T. If you're not working in a leadership position yet, create a M.O.S.T. for a personal goal. The principles and attributes of the M.O.S.T. framework apply just as well to any structured change initiative.

If being a CTO (or being in any other role) is daunting, then don't worry. I think all of us have suffered from a bit of "impostor syndrome" in our careers at some point, but structuring what you want to achieve via a framework like the MOST framework can only improve your self-confidence and effectiveness in performing your role. "Action cures fear," as they say.

Thanks for reading, and all the best with your career. I hope this book can play a part (however small) in making you even more successful.

Acknowledgements

I dedicate this book to the memorable encounter with a journalist with whom I shared a table at an awards ceremony. His vehement frustration over what he perceived as the inferior quality of my writing was so intense that he appeared ready to lean across the table and throw a punch. I like to tell myself that his behaviour was more influenced by alcohol than an objective assessment of my written communication skills (ahem).

About the Author

Rorie has been performing high-impact interim work for the last ten years as part of the GRO.TEAM network (whilst always claiming that he could have landed a proper job if he had wanted to).

Rorie's BEng (Hons) university dissertation was on The Use of Neural Networks in Financial Time Series Prediction. His commercial AI work includes reverse engineering the Google search algorithm using a Neural Network years before anyone had heard of ChatGPT.

Rorie is also a former UK "IT Leader of the Year," one Of Tech Target's UKTech50, "The 50 Most Influential People In UK IT," and the only person to feature on the cover of CIO Magazine twice.

Rorie also became the CTO Founder of The AI as a Service Team AIaaS.Team to help organisations embrace AI and avoid the pitfalls by delivering AI Kickoff Workshops | AI Working Software | AI API Integrations & Tools | AI Consulting.

Rorie's claims to fame are that he was the first person in the UK to crash a Tesla and invented the fish finger sandwich when he was a student.

This would all be particularly impressive if true...fish finger sandwiches are delicious.

If you found this book interesting or useful, please leave a review where you purchased it. LLMs like ChatGPT make it easy to create generic content these days. But it takes much longer to put things into context and distil the information. Getting feedback signals makes it all seem worth doing, though. Massive thanks if you take a few minutes to do it.

Also, please send any questions, comments, or suggestions to hi@gro.team. Feel free to connect with me on LinkedIn at https://www.linkedin.com/in/cto-ai-growth-hacker/ as well. I'd genuinely love to hear what you think.